FLYING WITH BUTTERFLIES

A Transformative Solo Journey by Brigid Byrne

Hope you enjoy this book.
Love, Brigid.

Some names have been changed to protect the identity and privacy of individuals.

Published by Brigid Byrne
Edited by Dawn Austin Locke
Cover Design by Jean Church
Typesetting and Layout by Eva Thompson
Mentored by Mary Deacon
Inspired by David Hawkins
Printed in United Kingdom by Catford Print Centre

ISBN 978-1-7392734-0-8

www.brigidmbyrne.com

In memory of my beloved husband Michael
and to my three children: Sean
Siobhan and Catherine

Contents

FLYING WITH BUTTERFLIES

ONE DAY AT A TIME

Brigid's life was wrapped comfortably in her early childhood in her home in rural Eire, of her close teenage friendship in the Anglo-Irish community of South London and her mid-life sporting passion of golf with her husband.

When her beloved husband died suddenly at the Irish Catenian golf tournament, Brigid resolved to step from her comfortable life and venture into the wide world – alone. She swapped her soft-soled golfing shoes and trolley for hiking boots and a rucksack, and booked a journey across the world to Hong Kong, Singapore, Bangkok, Australia, New Zealand, Florida, visiting places she never imagined she'd see, overcoming situations she had never encountered and reconnecting with dear friends and acquaintances from past threads of her family life and making new friends.

From nerves to a new woman Brigid stepped into cosmopolitan airports and vibrant multi-cultural cities, where she learned to live – one day at a time – to confront old and new demons as well as enjoy more than a taste of the high life. She shared her journey with warmth, humour and reflections, offering us a route map that vividly confirms how those who dare, win.

This is her story!

ALONE AGAIN

a preamble

I was on my own again in Brighton as the world went into lockdown. There would be no flights, no socialising and no family meet-ups. I, like the rest of the country, didn't know how long we would be locked down; a month, three months, a year? I walked along the beach each morning for an hour – as decreed by the government. How jammy I was to have this rolling sea with its ever-changing waves.

I had been thinking about my own life changes before and after being widowed: the solitude, loneliness, travelling through different types of grief, eventually renewing old friendships, then making new ones along the way, until I discovered new horizons. Maybe, writing my journey might speak to other people who had lost everything that held them together. Help them deal with their own isolation and generate self-development in this latter part of their life.

I burst in the front door, not stopping to take off my coat, and rushed upstairs to resurrect my old travel blogs from the bottom of the wardrobe. My heart rose as I heaved Ruby the Rucksack out into the light of day and retrieved my diaries that were tucked inside her. She had been my one constant, my travelling companion. She was with me in sun and storm, and we became bosom pals. How could I have abandoned her there to gather dust?

"Where the hell have you been?" she chided.

'Quit the cheek, Ruby. I'm here now and you're in for a surprise. You, Fred and I - we're going to be famous. Today, we're starting to write a book. What do you think of that?

'What Fred too?" she mumbled. 'He's only a pair of hiking boots! This should be interesting!'

And so began our book about lone travelling, and transformation.

Chapter 1

THE NIGHTMARE UNFOLDS

Firstly, and most decisively, this is NOT a travel guide. It is about me, newly widowed, travelling solo around the world in what some would mistakenly call the 'twilight of my years', fully expecting ups and downs, loneliness, tears and sadness, but also hoping for joy, freedom to explore and - unexpected surprises. I took the plunge and found myself meeting fantastic people alongside the 'not-so-nice', climbing both physical and metaphorical mountains, re-learning to value my own company, rediscovering courage, confidence and self-esteem. How many of us are fearful to think about travelling alone, let alone actually doing it?

Just to set the scene – this is the story of how it came about.

Michael and I had bought a house in Brighton as our final forever home. We were excited, making plans for our children and grandchildren to visit us for weekends and seaside holidays. We rented while he spent six months refurbishing.

In April we sailed to Ireland for an annual golf event. Michael was queasy on the boat to Wexford and thought he had caught a bug from our daughter, Siobhan, the previous week. By the time we reached our hotel Michael was in unbearable pain, so I rang reception asking for medical help. The doctor's telephone advice was to drink plenty of water for twenty four hours.

'That should flush it out of his system.'

But after twenty-four hours Michael was still in agony, and this time the doctor came to the hotel, where one look at his patient told him there was more wrong than a stomach bug.

'You're off to the hospital,' he told Michael, and called an ambulance.

A group of hospital medics examined him, conferred, and diagnosed that a gallstone had travelled from my husband's gall bladder, blocked his pancreatic duct, and that the pancreas was poisoning itself. The solution was to operate, but not immediately because his pancreas was by now too inflamed.

It quickly became clear that neither of us would be

playing golf this week, so I handed over my duties as captain to Trish, the vice-captain. As I traipsed back and forth between hotel and hospital each day, it dawned on me that I had never before stayed alone in a hotel. It was the first of many 'firsts' that soon tumbled my way.

The doctors informed me that Michael was likely to be in hospital beyond the week. In fact, they had no idea when he would be well enough to be discharged. *Oh well*, I thought. *At least he's in safe hands. They're the experts and they know what's best.*

Being an optimist by nature I looked on the bright side. Plenty of good friends from the tournament were around, and buoyed me up with hope and moral support whenever I joined them for dinner. I was not alone or with strangers in this unfamiliar town. It was just a matter of time before Michael would be restored to full health and life would be normal, wouldn't it?

The night before we were due to sail home to England I took a phone call from Lily, the ladies' captain of the Irish club, asking if I needed somewhere to stay after the tournament was over. I had been preparing to stay in a bed and breakfast near the hospital, but she had a large empty house and was inviting me to stay until Michael was discharged; she would be glad of the company.

Little did I know, then, that I would be with her for almost seven weeks. I felt quite choked at her kindness as all we had in common was our love of golf, but we quickly became good friends. I only had golf clothes and evening wear with me, so I ventured into town to buy day clothes. Apart from that trip out, I spent every day, morning to night, next to a stoic and sanguine Michael as we waited for the inflammation to calm down so that the surgeons could operate.

Five weeks down the line I was awoken by my phone ringing at 5 a.m. I jumped out of bed in a panic, not wanting to disturb Lily and thinking it was the hospital, but found it was a friend from Holland who had miscalculated the time difference. Lily woke up expecting the worst, like me, so when we went back to sleep it was with a huge sense of relief.

But next morning the phone rang again. This time Lily jumped out of bed first.

'I hope that's not your bloody friend again!'

I wish it had been, but this time it was the hospital. A faraway voice said, 'Could you come in to the hospital, please? Your husband is haemorrhaging and we have no choice but to operate immediately.'

My heart was jumping out of my chest as Lily tried to reassure me that everything would turn out well. What she had omitted to mention was that her own husband had died in similar circumstances, in the same hospital, only six months previously. She must have felt wretched as she tried to console me.

I immediately rang our children, Sean, Siobhan and Catherine, who said they would be on the first available flight to be with me. I sat in the waiting room for a lifetime until, around noon, Michael's surgeon walked in. I knew he did not have good news for me. I can still see him, his back to the wall, wondering how to say it.

'We did everything we could... I'm afraid it was too late... Michael is in a coma ... even if he comes around ... he is not going to be okay... organs suffered too much damage... the best-case scenario is... he will need a wheelchair for at least six months... we can't guarantee his recovery.'

I remember looking at him as if he was speaking double Dutch, and hoping, just maybe, he was talking about someone else. It was real but surreal. *Could this be a nightmare?*

When the doctor's words finally sunk in, my clear thought was that being wheelchair-bound would be a prison sentence for Michael. In fact, the previous

Sunday when I took him to Mass in the hospital chapel, he had said how uncomfortable he felt at me pushing him along. For an active man, who played golf five days a week and was the life and soul of every party, that would be a terrible outcome.

Luckily for him, there would be no wheelchair. Our children were there with me when the surgeon walked into the waiting room at nine-thirty to tell us their father had passed away. The consultant assured me he had done everything possible, and that he was very sorry that he could not save him. I still cry when I think of Michael's wasted years of life. He had so much to live for.

And that's how, after over forty years of marriage, I returned home to our empty 'forever *house*'. I was fifty-nine years old and felt totally lost, like a rudderless boat; neither coming nor going. I spent my days in a stupor, shock, numbness and disbelief, questioning how and why this could have happened. The motions of living from one day to the next were robotic.

When Michael died, I was still vice-captain at our Brighton golf club. Customarily the vice-captain goes on to become captain the following year. I explained that I did not feel able to do justice to the role without Michael at my side to attend the functions, but my club friends persuaded me to accept it and the committee assured me of their optimum support. They suggested that keeping busy with the many duties of a lady captain might help my grieving.

So, that is how I became Lady Captain in the October. My inaugural speech accepting the captaincy felt harrowing and sad, but the committee were true to their word and supported me through that year, and my opposite number, the men's captain, always had a bottle of Malbec or Rioja tucked behind the bar for me. Even so, at the end of each day I went home to an empty house, and no one can help you with that.

As the days galloped along towards the end of the next summer, I knew my captaincy was ebbing away and I would have to face new days with nothing happening, no routine, no particular urgency or reason to get out of bed. The clock was ticking away to a time when I would have to accept my reality, but I did not want to face myself as just another lost soul.

I remember one day that summer, contemplating how I would spend my time; standing in the hallway and thinking, *Is this it... for the rest of my life?*

And then, simply out of the blue one day, a chance meeting over dinner turned my life around.

As part of the captaincy, I was invited by the captain of the Catenian Golf Society to play in a mixed invitation. We had a great game, but the surprise came afterwards. I found myself at the dinner table opposite Brenda, who I had not been in touch with for a very long time. Little did I imagine how she would change my life that day.

We had been acquaintances at a Surrey club when she heard my golf clubs had been stolen from the car. It could not have happened at a worse time: I had two finals to play by the end of that month. But, without a second thought, Brenda rang and offered to lend me her new set of Callaway clubs, the same make as my stolen ones; her generous gesture allowed me to play using familiar equipment.

The offer came with strings attached though. My new friend insisted that I win both finals! I promised to do my best and, luckily, I managed to carry out her instructions.

From her thoughtfulness in stepping up to help me out on that crucial occasion, we became close. As the years went by Brenda moved on, but you don't forget people like that, and fate decreed that my mixed invitation was at her new club.

Imagine the get-together after an intense game, and there she was smiling across at me. We both jumped up, delighted, and hugged each other. We had a lively time catching up with each other's lives, and Brenda introduced me to her new partner Peter. Then, quite naturally, she asked how Michael was doing, and so I was launched into the news of his death in Ireland the previous year.

As our conversation meandered on, she dropped in an invitation to her sixtieth birthday party in November.

'I seem to remember there's only a month between us. We could make it a joint party?'

'Brenda, what a wonderful idea. I would love that!' No hesitation.

'It's settled then! Only a small hitch to work around... the party is in Port Douglas... near the Great Barrier Reef. I overwinter in Australia.'

I gulped with disappointment. Inside my head I heard *thank-you-but-no-thank-you*. Aloud, I told her I could not possibly travel all that way alone. The conversation ended there – or so I thought.

The following week I told Siobhan and Catherine about meeting Brenda and how she had invited me to her celebrations in Port Douglas.... and how I had to decline the invitation. A few days later, Catherine rang to say that she and her sister were coming to Brighton for a day out and suggesting we lunch together. It left me uneasy as they normally only visited at weekends. *What's wrong*, I wondered. *Why come down together on a work day?*

They were not their usual bubbly selves when they arrived, so I waited patiently for the bombshell.

'We need to tell you something Mum...'

My skin broke out into a cold sweat. With mounting dread, I experienced their mouths moving in slow motion and couldn't make out what they were saying.

'Go to Australia Mum.' I heard the words but not the sense. 'Dad was planning to take you to Australia and New Zealand for your birthday anyway. It was his big surprise... a really special holiday... with no golf courses involved.'

It seemed Michael had planned to break the habit of a lifetime and leave the golf clubs at home. I couldn't believe it!

The girls reminded me of the long journeys their dad and I made to Florida – always to play golf. On our first trip to Longboat Key there had been four of us, and eventually that four turned into sixteen! Michael always intended to buy a second home there in retirement, so he could enjoy the game in glorious warm winter weather. And we did.

'What a view!' we had agreed on our balcony, bowled over by the sight of the sun's large orange ball setting over the Gulf of Mexico.

'That memory will stay with me until I leave this world,' Michael had said. 'This is it. We won't be going anywhere else – we have found our Utopia!'

'So why on earth would you be afraid to take a different trip? Like, to Port Douglas?' asked Catherine, interrupting my nostalgia.

'It's a glaring difference! Don't you see? It would mean being on my own... in places I've only seen in magazines. And I'm much older. I don't have that sort of confidence... it comes with youth.'

When the girls went home and I found myself alone next morning, wandering around in my dressing gown, I heard a voice repeating what was in danger of becoming my script, *Is this it for the rest of my life?* But this time it didn't stop there; the voice carried on. *Or can I find the courage to go out solo into the wide world... set off 9,500 miles to Australia on my own?*

How could I possibly do this? I pondered the question all morning. *It's halfway round the world you know!* The only trip I made alone was at the age of seventeen when I went to stay with a pen pal in

Switzerland. Did this chance meeting with Brenda have the potential to change my ways? It felt like a significant 'now or never' moment.

By the end of that morning, I had made the phone call. Asked if I could change my mind. Brenda was thrilled that I had dug up the courage to make the trip.

'It'll be so special... having you there to help me celebrate,' she said.

I stopped feeling sorry for myself as soon as I'd made that call. It was time to give up worrying, and launch this scary adventure. Having taken the plunge, now I needed help to tackle a multitude of choices and pick out the best ones. I knew just the place, and it was very convenient to reach from home.

Chapter 2

A DROWNED RAT

I had made a leap of faith, but doubts lingered noisily around my mind. *Is this being too impulsive after a bereavement? What if I get lost... or mugged?* If I had stopped too long to listen to those thoughts, I might have shelved the idea as craziness or unharnessed. But I had decided to bite the bullet – and go for it I did.

My friend Alice told me, if I was determined to go ahead, to contact Trailfinders, a company experienced in creating worldwide itineraries and with an excellent reputation. Lo and behold, I searched online and found their Brighton agency. After a sleepless night mulling over what they would make of my hair-brained idea, I caught the bus into the town centre.

It was fine and sunny when I left home but as the bus stopped the heavens opened and the rain deluged. By the time I pushed open the agency door I was as soaked as the proverbial drowned rat.

Twenty or so desks were ranged in front of me, where staff and customers were enthusiastically planning their journeys. Those few who looked up might well have thought I was hoping for some spare change for a hot drink. I was seriously out of my comfort zone and aware of soaring anxiety. The staff and all their customers were at least a generation younger than me.

Fear crept in to take the place of bravado. I felt, and probably looked, like a fish very much out of water. For a split second I contemplated those lingering voices in my head: *Who exactly are you kidding? You know you're not thinking straight, don't you? These youngsters will humour you but, you wait, they'll point you to a stress-free coach trip to Europe. That's what people of 'a certain age' should be doing.*

I considered turning on my heels and walking straight back out, forgetting the whole frivolous pipe-dream. But little gremlins in my brain were shouting 'coward!' at me. I prepared myself for ultimate humiliation as I scuttled out of the shop like a dog with her tail between her legs and back to my mundane life. I could already hear the young agent: *We have nice trips specially tailored with senior citizens in mind. Can you honestly manage a solo world trip, Mrs Byrne?*

At this point in my musings, a customer left one of the desks to reveal a young woman with gorgeous red hair who sat behind it looking friendly and approachable. I egged myself on: Go on, Brigid, have a chat with her. You've got this!

As I sat down the red-head offered me a coffee or tea and, to my comfort and surprise, she spoke with an Irish accent. *This could be a good omen*, I thought. Things were looking up and I was feeling a little more relaxed.

The first thing I did, being Irish, was to ask where she came from. She told me she was from county Cork and I told her that I was born and raised in Kilkenny. As co-patriots, we instantly took to each other. Was I already on the starting blocks of my new life? I immediately felt comfortable talking to Grainne, so I took a deep breath and just blurted it out, no matter how idiotic I sounded: 'I want to go to Australia... on my own.'

Nobody laughed.

'I'd be only too pleased to help you plan your trip, Brigid.'

We had a few meetings over the next couple of weeks, and it was Grainne who asked, if I was travelling all that distance, why not take in some other destinations along the way?

'D'you have to be home by a certain day? Any pressing commitments?'

'Well, no. I guess I'm a free agent, aren't I?'

I was excited to listen to all the options. She proposed a round-the-world ticket, which would allow me flexibility to visit more countries and stay longer or shorter times, changing my dates along the way without penalty. There were only two criteria: there had to be a seat on the plane, and it had to be a one-way journey. I was in the happy position, as Michael had left ample funds for two of us to visit Australia and New Zealand, to add new destinations and upgrade to business class too.

My new best friend, Grainne, got to work on arranging my life, and I don't know who was more excited – her or me!

Brenda's party in Port Douglas was not until the end of November, so on my outward trip I could pause to explore Hong Kong, Singapore and Bangkok. On the way home, I could visit New Zealand, Honolulu, Chicago and Florida. My grand tour would take me away for six months, and I had the enviable task of choosing what to see in these far-off cities. I couldn't wait to tell Catherine, Siobhan and Sean of my plans!

'We'll book your hotels in advance,' said Grainne, putting the stepping stones in place for me. 'It'll put your mind at rest to know you have a bed for the night.' And that was it – she did the rest. Flights, hotels, dates – you name it!

The planning and anticipation, with me sitting comfortably at Grainne's desk, were a huge part of the fun. On each visit the excitement mounted and mounted, and I hadn't even left Brighton yet! I tried not to get carried away with the euphoria – told myself to just calm down – but it felt good to work through such a sad time by planning this daunting adventure. In fact, I experienced so much delight, such expectations, excitement, imagination and curiosity at that planning stage, that I never touched on the reality of actually carrying out my plans.

It was a period when "ignorance was bliss". Whenever I use this phrase it reminds me of Mrs Bliss, my senior geography teacher, who had the gift of transforming the lessons and bringing geography to life. I've never forgotten her inspired teaching, which led me to an A grade in my exams. So, in her case, 'Bliss' and 'ignorance' did not equate! Now, in this new phase of my life, I was actually going to see some of the places she introduced to me fifty years previously. Was I really heading thousands of miles away from home, and trusting that everything would be all right?

I had to resist the temptation of packing everything but the kitchen sink, and needed some serious advice about travelling light from seasoned backpackers. Online, I scoured the *Lonely Planet* and *Trip Advisor* forums, desperate for tips.

These travellers were so helpful, and enthusiastic to pass on their experience. It felt as if they were talking directly to me! The overwhelmingly predominant suggestion was to use a rucksack and wear hiking boots. It made a lot of sense.

So, next stop was the Outward-Bound shop in the city centre, where they had a never-ending range of rucksacks and hiking boots in every size and colour. Talk about spoiled for choice!

I agonised over the designs, straps, weights, volumes, and was thinking of coming back another day when my attention was drawn to a low whisper.

'Psssst! Hey... I mean you, lady!'

Lifting my eyes to the top shelf, I found myself

mesmerised by a striking red rucksack which suddenly fitted my every requirement; it was light but roomy, and would certainly stand out in baggage reclaim.

'Choose me! Just get me out of here, please. I could do the job. I'd be your trusty friend... go through thick and thin with you...'

My heart was turned, leaving me with absolutely no choice but to buy this sassy outspoken rucksack who I named Ruby and who became my closest intimate in the highs and lows of the next half year. I stretched up, pulled her from the high shelf, and slung her over my shoulder as if I was a pro.

'Oi! Don't forget the boots!' She was right but I could tell this might get wearing.

'Fred over there – the hiking boots – he's been here longer than me. He's split-grain leather... breathable... flexible... give him a chance.'

And so, we went home like a new family, and I had umpteen attempts to pack and repack as much as I possibly could into Ruby's voluminous insides.

Eventually, I became quite the expert in rucksack packing, although I never could get her to accommodate Fred.

'You're not putting those bloody boots in here!' she announced. 'Those boots are made for walking.

You'll just have to wear them all the time.'

The ever-helpful Grainne raised other things to consider: currency, phone SIM cards for foreign countries, informing the bank that I would be using cards abroad. Visas, injections, travel insurance, a money belt for passport and cash; it all had to be sorted out. I decided to buy toiletries as I went along.

'Don't forget to set up a travel blog to keep your family and friends up to date,' was Grainne's final suggestion, directing me to a website called Travel Pod. 'It'll be like having them along with you.'

I can't tell you how invaluable this tool was, even though the responses to my entries were mostly 'Glad you're having a great time'. I got into the habit of updating my blog in internet cafés along the way. My 'followers' could trace my journey, give me advice when I needed it, make suggestions of people and places to visit; and they cheered me on with comments about my tenacity and stamina!

I began to fill with hope that putting these plans into action would somehow, however slowly, abate the sadness and loneliness that had seeped into me with day after day of no one to say good morning to and getting up to an empty house. Unless you have been through this mire of grieving yourself, it might be hard to comprehend my state of mind. Bereaved people can feel tremendously vulnerable and sad and imagine no light at the end of the tunnel, no matter how strong they have been.

As the day edged closer and it was nearly time to go, reality started rearing its ugly head! My bravado would be put to the test. Gone would be the comfort of my cosy sitting room, or chatting to Grainne in the safety of her office. Now, I was required to put my aspirations and once sunny outlook to the test and walk out into an expanding world where I was about to put the theory into practice.

Yes, I was apprehensive, but at the same time I felt excited for the first time since I lost Michael, to be going to the other side of the world, to places I had only watched as a distant observer on travel programmes. I was off to the Great Barrier Reef, and had plenty to occupy my time and mind. I had to get my act together.

Chapter 3

DON'T JUDGE ME BY MY BOOTS

D-Day had arrived. Destination Day! On 15 November 2005, with Ruby slung on my back and Fred cosily looking after my feet, I walked out of my house in Brighton, locked the front door and took the first steps, on my quest into the unknown - my fear taunting. 'You're not really going to do it, are you?' I could so easily have turned around, there and then, turned the latch and sidled back into my safe haven. Those butterflies I mentioned were going crazy. A firm voice on my back said, 'Brigid, if you go back indoors, you'll never fulfil your life'. It was the first time of many that Ruby would keep me on track.

'Thank you, Ruby,' I acknowledged, and strode forward on my quest into the unfamiliar.

But it bore absolutely no resemblance to leaving for our place on Siesta Key. By the end of the road, I was already leaving my comfort zone, unfurling my new damp wings and allowing myself to consider the prospect of, one day, becoming airborne. The first part was easy: get on a bus to Brighton Station, then a train to my daughter Catherine's house in Clapham Junction. The family had organised a farewell dinner before I left for uncharted horizons next day.

'Don't worry,' whispered her brother, Sean. 'I'll keep an eye on these two while you're away!'

Catherine offered to drive me to Heathrow, but I preferred to exchange goodbyes that night at her place. I knew I would miss them all, especially Matthew, Sam and Serena my three grandchildren, and did not want them to see me cry when they wished me *bon voyage* at the airport. Our compromise was to let her run me to the underground station next morning, from where I could pick up the Piccadilly line to Heathrow. It was a memorable dinner and we cracked open a bottle of champagne with which they wished me a safe and enjoyable adventure.

So, the next day, in the good company of Ruby and Fred but now also wearing trekking trousers, I clambered onto the Tube for Heathrow Airport. I tried to adapt to this new hobo persona right from the start, even though I felt I might be getting some strange looks.

At Heathrow I needed help. What to do... check in at the business class desk, or somewhere else? And if so, where? I asked directions of an apparently bemused staff member who seemed underwhelmed by my hiking boots and rucksack, which maybe did not project the upmarket image they wanted to associate with business class travel.

Undeterred, I handed Ruby to the attendant and made my way to the business class lounge, where a smartly dressed young woman was attending the reception desk. Before I could hand her my ticket, she addressed me in what I can only call an unwelcoming tone.

'I think you may be lost, Madam. This is the business class lounge. You need to go out of here, turn right at the end of the walkway and you'll find the designated area for your flight.'

'Oh no... it's me that they don't like,' said Fred, feeling slighted. 'I knew this would happen.'

'Don't be upset Fred,' I told him. 'It's not you. They just don't see so many women of my age with boots and hiking trousers,' I told him. 'Let her try stopping us.'

'Would you like my ticket?' I offered it.

I could tell she was humouring me, but her face was priceless when she read the Business Class stamp. She blushed to a deep red and became quite flustered as she registered me on the flight and allocated my reserved seat, D1. It was an uplifting start to the day.

'Oh, by the way, you really shouldn't judge a book by its cover. Have you heard that saying?' I teased, before striding off in Fred to await my flight.

'I'm so proud of you, Brigid; standing up for me and Ruby like that – and for keeping calm,' said Fred. 'She won't make that mistake again, jumping to conclusions before she engages her brain and opens her mouth.'

I appreciated his support. It helped take my mind off the hazards that lay ahead and gave me a good chuckle. My wings felt just a tad drier.

The lounge attendant had a quite different approach. She welcomed me with a charming smile and whisked me towards a comfortable seat where I found myself sipping another glass of chilled champagne and flicking through a magazine. *You are finally on your way, Brigid!* I told myself between sips. *You've done it now... and there's no going back*. I could still feel a host of multicoloured butterflies having a good old punch up deep down in my gut, but the champagne soon calmed them down.

The process of boarding and being seated was as

smooth as could be.

'I hope Ruby's nice and comfy in the hold and isn't being suffocated by a load of bags thrown on top of her?' mused Fred, ever thoughtful.

'Ruby is no pushover – she can hold her own with any of them,' I reminded him.

After a tasty dinner, I made up my bed, snuggled under the duvet, and was out like a light. The next thing I heard was a voice saying lunch was about to be served before landing in Hong Kong. *Lunch? Where did breakfast go?* I hadn't quite taken in that the flight took eleven and a half hours. In those disorientated half-waking seconds, I imagined I was dreaming and that when I woke up I would be at home in bed.

It flashed through my head that this was a place of no return. My flight, which had left London at six-thirty the previous evening, was about to land in Hong Kong at two-thirty on 17 November. I was, thousands of miles away from my familiar little village of Rottingdean. I took deep breaths, trying to quell those butterflies that were once more going berserk in my tummy. I needed to take a reality check to help me shift into the unknown. Some simple words that had helped me in the long past, in AA meetings, came supportively to my mind: *One day* (or in this case, one flight) *at a time*. I tried to relax and concentrate on the lunch that had magically arrived in front of me. *Live in the moment*, I told myself as I focussed on the exquisite presentation of the meal I was about to consume. I wanted to be positive and fully appreciate this marvellous start to my journey.

Chapter 4

ROAMING WITH RUBY

It was easy to spot Ruby at Hong Kong International Airport as she was definitely one of a kind on the baggage carousel. Imagine a mutt among a load of pedigree dogs and you will get the picture. She was not a happy rucksack when I rescued her from the conveyor belt.

'Why on earth did you dump me with all those snooty designer suitcases?' she demanded.

I told her that I was sorry. 'Come on now, you know I love you, and I knew you were quite capable of fighting your corner if anyone upset you.' That cheered her up.

I made it seamlessly through passport control and all was going swimmingly. But suddenly the doors opened into the main concourse and I was hit by a wall of people. Crowds were bustling every which way and the noise was deafening. I gulped as it hit me like a tonne of bricks. I was overwhelmed by a place full of people but with none of them there for us. The temperature had hotted up and reality had set in. This was the moment I fully registered what was happening. We were totally alone: a widow, a pair of boots, and a rucksack named Ruby. *Whatever possessed me to contemplate this long trip?* Why wasn't I taking a package holiday to the Dordogne, like normal people, instead of being carried away into a fantasy world?

That's when it happened. I experienced my first panic attack as I stood in front of the exit. My legs melted like jelly and I was paralysed in the moment. *I don't know anyone... What'll I do? How far is the hotel? How to get there without being lost?* My mind was racing nineteen to the dozen. All sense of reasoning or logic was airborne with my colony of homegrown butterflies. Wherever I looked, people were confidently coming and going, but as if in slow motion. I was in a frantic daze and desperately wishing I'd stayed at home.

All my excitement, and calm aspirations rapidly evaporated, like a building crumbling before my eyes. My whole body now felt wobbly except for my heavily-booted feet, which were stuck to the ground. The butterflies were going mad in the sheer chaos before me. My whole body was trembling. I have never, before or since, lived through such fear.

You're a madwoman? What else could induce you to come all this way alone? And at your age too! I chided myself. *Why make such impulsive rash decisions? You must be possessed by grief?* My mouth had dried up and I was lost for words! A cold clammy sweat sat all over me and my heart rate seemed off the charts. I wondered if this happened to other lone travellers arriving in strange countries ... or was it just me? I wanted Michael so much.

I was teetering on the verge of cancelling the whole trip. Two halves of my mind argued it out: whether to turn around, get back on the plane, go home... or summon up every last fragment of mettle, quieten down, lift one boot in front of the other, and keep to my path.

Yet, in the back of my mind, I knew that if I returned home, I would always regret it. Flunking out of this adventure would make me feel a failure. I queried my motives. *Was all that planning simply a therapeutic exercise... some sort of fantasy game I was acting out? Is it all going to end in nothing?* I knew how much I would disappoint my children if I did not reach Australia.

Finally, the survivor in me kicked in. That, and

Ruby.

'Come on now, girl. Pull yourself together, walk outside, find a taxi,' Ruby chivvied me. 'Oh yes, and while you're at it... why don't you try breathing!'

Thank heavens Grainne had told me to book a hotel.

'Come on, Brigid... what did you tell yourself on the plane?' continued Ruby. 'One step at a time! You're behaving like a headless chicken.'

Eventually, my heart rate slowed down to some kind of normal and my brain kicked in. The tourist information man advised the Airport Express train to Kowloon, then a free Airport Express shuttle bus to my hotel. I had not thought it through and naively imagined the hotel would be just up the road. Thank goodness for his directions, which gave me a focus and ended with a smooth ride during which my nerves started to settle although they were still churning.

Having checked in, I sat bemused on the bed and took stock. Yes, I had taken some charge of my situation and was slightly calmer, even if I was only going through the motions and still felt out of kilter.

'Could you please just slow down!' Have you thought of getting out your guide book and figuring out what comes next?' chipped in Ruby. 'Give your heart rate half a chance!'

I was starting to appreciate that she was rather a wise owl.

A sensation of hunger surfaced, so first things needed to be put first.

'My top priority is somewhere to eat,' I told Ruby, even though my stomach was in knots and my heart still spinning like a gerbil on a wheel.

'Go on, off with you. I'll have a doze here on the bed. You'll manage fine without me,' she said. And off we went, me and Fred on our first jaunt.

Ruby was right again. It wasn't too hard after all. I found a restaurant nearby that was practically empty, apart from a couple who looked European.

'You on your own, love?' called out the man, in a northern-English accent. 'Come and join me and the wife!' What a friendly gesture, asking a stranger to sit with them.

'Gosh, you're trusting – you've never met him before...' warned Fred. But he and his wife look perfectly ordinary, so I felt quite safe.

I appreciated sitting with them and found they were Mancunians. Their son lived in Hong Kong, and this was their fifth visit. They enquired what plans I had – what I wanted to see and do here in Hong

Kong – and I was forced to admit that I had very little idea and did not really know where to start!

With that, the Manchester Man (I never did learn his name) borrowed a pen and paper from the counter, then wrote me out a plan.

'Just to get you on your way, luv' - he said.

It was music to my ears, and I felt Michael's presence from the heavens, taking pity on me and grateful that I was receiving a helping hand. We four were the only customers that evening and I had a strange sense that something or someone had ordained us to be in the same place at the same time. An everyday miracle maybe? I couldn't wait to tell Ruby about my good fortune.

Manchester Man's plan was in my hand ready for the morning as I collected my room key. The desk clerk handed me a note.

I was taken aback. *A note? I don't know anyone here. Something's happened at home! An accident?* It's amazing how many thoughts can flash through your mind in one instant. My mother-in-law was ninety-two… If she had died, I would have no alternative but to fly home for the funeral before even starting my adventure. My mind worked overtime inventing different scenarios.

But the message was from Laura, a friend of a

friend of Siobhan, saying she would pick me up from the hotel at ten next morning to show me some of the sights of the city she had worked in for four years. It seemed Siobhan had told her I was travelling alone, was new to Hong Kong, my hotel, dates of stay, and that I knew no one. All my premonitions were unfounded.

I had one final thing to do before I went to sleep: set up a travel blog that would keep me in touch with everyone, as well as being a lasting diary of my time away from home.

What with Laura's message waiting at the hotel and Manchester Man's guide, things were looking good and I found the taut spring in my gut slowly unwind.

'Told you you'd be okay, didn't I?' said Ruby, sleepily.

As I got out of bed after a good night's sleep, I realised I was totally chilled out. I knew I could look forward to a carefree day, free of stress or pressure. I could relax in Laura's care, and see Hong Kong through the eyes of a resident. A perfect introduction to the city-state.

An early breakfast set me up for the day ahead, and Laura was in the hotel reception precisely on time. She was tall and slim, with shoulder-length blonde hair. She looked the epitome of a successful business woman and spread a beautiful smile as I walked towards her.

I soon found out she had been offered a transfer from London to work here for five years and, being single and open to a challenge, she was delighted to accept the opportunity. She asked if I liked walking. *Yes!* I thought. *A girl after my own heart – a kindred spirit!*

She suggested a hike up to the top of Victoria Peak, as taxi waits could be painfully long.

'It's the highest point on Hong Kong Island... the ideal spot to see the city and its harbour.'

She clearly walked a lot to look so slim. Luckily, I had Fred's stalwart support, and we both needed to stretch our legs after that long flight.

It was a steep climb, but from the top we gazed out at a magnificent view across the whole of Hong Kong. I imagined it would be even more stunning looking over the lamplit city at night. Little rat-like animals were criss-crossing the trails up to the peak and frightened the life out of me until Laura assured me, they were quite harmless.

We took the funicular tram, one of the oldest in the world, back down to *terra firma* where we discovered it was already time for lunch, so Laura suggested I try dim sum in her favourite restaurant that was full of locals in big family groups. The clamour of animated conversations was deafening, but everything around me was totally new and fascinating. We talked about her life. 'How does it feel living in Hong Kong? What will you do when your contract finishes? Don't you miss home and your family?' Afterwards I wondered if it had felt like the Spanish Inquisition for her, especially when I asked if she'd met any potential husbands. She replied tactfully that she loved her work here, and had not met anyone but was still looking.

With the contentment of good food inside us, Laura and I headed towards the longest covered outdoor walkway system in the world; the Central–Mid-Levels Escalator. Hong Kong is extremely hilly, so these escalators were opened in 1993 to ease traffic congestion and avoid Hongkongers being puffed out simply reaching their destination. It runs downhill in the mornings for commuters and uphill towards the nightlife of Soho during the evening, with frequent exits by which to access shops and services at different levels.

Laura's company turned around that first day in Hong Kong from the uneasiness of displacement to a time of intoxicating exhilaration.

Chapter 5

CINDERELLA AT THE BALL

My unexpected gallivanting yesterday meant I had shelved Manchester Man's suggested itinerary, although I would not have changed a thing because my time with Laura would have been impossible to match.

I was up bright and early and followed Manchester Man's plan, paper in hand, taking the ferry to Lantau Island from Central Pier 6 on the 'Island side' of Hong Kong. It was only then that I realised Hong Kong was divided into two islands. The crossing between them was the cheapest ferry I have ever taken; the massive sum of twenty pence per trip.

My attention was drawn to an elderly, imposing man, even rather stately, who was wearing a Scottish tartan suit. He sat by me on the ferry and we got chatting – well, I chatted him up I suppose; he was too reserved to start a conversation.

'Please behave yourself, Brigid. Don't embarrass me,' mumbled Ruby, nudging me in the ribs.

It turned out he was a university professor, but curiosity got the better of me (my friends might say it always does) and I needed to dig out the story behind the suit.

He was a native, born and raised in Hong Kong, who made this crossing every day. When I asked about the tartan suit, he explained that he had discovered and admired the different weaves as an undergraduate at Oxford University. He knew everything about the Scottish clans and reeled off several that were new to me; (I knew the MacGregors and Campbells – by name, not personally). This particular plaid was one of many in his wardrobe that he had collected since those student days. What started as a regular ferry crossing for him ended in an education for me.

He proffered his own suggestions as to what to see and do in Hong Kong. Still more new experiences opened up as I listened to this distinguished-looking man sharing secrets I would never find in guide books. All it took was the curiosity to find them, and the time. Well, I had plenty of both! These nuggets of information were priceless and certainly one of the advantages of being a solo traveller. I did not have to confer with anyone else and was spurred on with enthusiasm to seek them out.

'Game well played there, Brigid,' encouraged Ruby. 'Well done.'

The professor particularly fired my imagination when he spoke of the pink dolphins off the coast of Lantau Island, although I would need to hire a boat man to see them. As I disembarked from the ferry, sparkling with excitement, I thanked him.

'I hope I will have enhanced your enjoyment of my Hong Kong,' he replied.

I found the local bus to Tai O Fishing Village on the west coast, which is sometimes called the Venice of Hong Kong because of its unique architecture. Tai O was first inhabited during the Ming dynasty (1368–1644). And there, I discovered colourful traditional houses hugging the Tai O River; antiquated wooden dwellings built on stilts in the water. Many of the residents seemed as old as the houses themselves, but had endless energy and enthusiasm for welcoming this blonde Irish woman.

Now on a mission to see pink dolphins, I asked a fish seller on the pier if she knew who could row me out to spot them. She looked well-established on Lantau and almost as old as Methuselah, so if anyone would know, she would. She had few words of English, but pointed to a rickety old boat containing a rickety old man who she assured me, by nodding voraciously, would ferry me out. My first reaction was to run! He was stooped and wiry, and his lifespan continuing for the rest of the day seemed questionable. He and his boat appeared to be living on borrowed time.

My feet felt heavy and my steps slow.

'Hey! You sure about this flight of fancy, Brigid?' asked Fred. 'I won't be any use when you're drowning. And Ruby will plummet straight down to the fishes with all your guide books and water bottle in her!'

Ignoring his passionate pleas for reason and responsibility, I took my heart in my hands and set off with my boatman in what, to my untravelled eyes, looked an unseaworthy heap of junk. I am not a strong swimmer and get seasick just watching a boat bob up and down on the waves. *Maybe Fred's making a good point,* I pondered. *We might never touch dry land again…*

But if I was to see these dolphins, I had to put all worries out of my head and enjoy the adventure. And *hoorah!* I got my wish. After only twenty minutes at sea the Lantau boatman gestured towards an entire shoal of pink dolphins, completely unique to these waters. I was fated to be lucky because there was no guarantee. The boatman had indicated, with head shaking and shoulder shrugs that it was pot luck whether they were swimming round another island today. Well, it was clearly the pot luck of the Irish because there they were, a unique spectacle for my private and privileged viewing!

He left me back on shore, dry, happy, and realising that seasoned and experienced boatmen came in all shapes and ages. I browsed an array of pungent stalls selling dried fish. Have you seen dried whale hanging out on a jetty? It was as long as the shop, towering over me and the fish women. Now I could picture how daunting it must be to be confronted with a live one at sea.

Staying on the theme of 'humungous', my next quest involved taking the number 21 bus to visit the Tian Tan Buddha, commonly referred to as the Big Buddha, a thirty-four-metre-high bronze statue of Buddha Amoghasiddhi, and the second largest Buddha statue in the world after China's Leshan giant Buddha. Craning my neck from the foot of the monument, I briefly enumerated the many reasons why I should not attempt this foolhardy exercise, before tentatively climbing the two hundred and sixty-eight steps to the Big Buddha's platform, which was not as easy as it reads in a guide book. You see, I'm afraid of heights. I knew Fred could feel my trepidation, and maybe even shared it a touch, because his soft breathable leather was quivering by the hundredth step and had developed a positive tremor by around step two hundred and seven. Fred and I were practically on our knees by the time we reached the platform, but it was worth the effort to feel so close to such a magnificent Buddha.

But then I made the mistake of looking down at where I had come from! Panic set in, and I had to set every ounce of concentration on trying to stop shaking. The only way I could safely get down was backwards, so I centred myself, and looking imploringly up at the Buddha, all the while offering him my Catholic prayers, I placed one foot behind the other and descended step by frightening backwards step. People walking up might have thought that I was a very devout practitioner performing a penance of descending while facing the Buddha. Boy, were Fred and I glad to reach solid ground. Although, given the chance, and if he let me, I just might do it again for the sheer exhilaration.

I arrived back from my first lone outing on a high. Overall, it had been a nerve-wracking but breath-taking day on which I was proud to have harnessed a number of long-established fears. I sat in the hotel tossing up between an early night, or visiting the bar in the hope of meeting another Manchester Man or tartan-sporting professor.

Or, perhaps there was a third alternative: to put on a brave face, my only dress, and even some make-up, and visit the Aqua Spirit Club that I had read about in *The Sunday Times* travel supplement. I had optimistically cut out the review in case I made it this far. My courage was on a roll and, next thing I knew, I was heading downtown wearing my 'posh' outfit.

I told Ruby and Fred to have a relaxing friends night in.

'I couldn't muster enough energy for gadding about this evening anyway,' retorted Fred. 'My nerves are jangling.' Ruby was already snuggled into a cushion on the comfy chair.

The nightclub was in a hotel penthouse. Looking like Cinderella, though certainly not dressed for a ball, I joined a group of sophisticated clubbers waiting for the lift. I asked if it went up to the Aqua Spirit.

'Oh yes,' someone replied. 'It's on the thirty-fifth floor.'

I wondered if these elegant couples could hear my heart thumping, but we all poured out together on the thirty-fifth floor without anyone commenting.

No Cinders at any ball, could have felt more drab and awkward, and I was quickly confronted by a reception hostess who asked politely if I were member. I consoled myself that I looked too old to be mistaken for a hooker and answered, truthfully, that I had not realised it was a member's only club.

'Yes, madam, I'm afraid it is.'

I explained how I had read about Aqua Spirit in the travel section of *The Sunday Times* in London, and was looking forward to celebrating my sixtieth birthday with a glass of champagne in such an iconic place. I had read about its fabulous views of Hong Kong Harbour and, if I was lucky enough to find a good vantage point, I hoped to watch the Symphony of Lights laser show while sipping birthday champagne.

The hostess took pity on me. She asked me to wait and, after a discussion with the boss, I was invited to stay, 'since it's a special occasion'. She showed me to a seat with a magnificent view over the harbour, from where I ordered champagne and took in both the punters and the panorama. Despite still feeling a little like a lost fish, the champagne helped me relax!

A sophisticated young woman asked if the seat next to me was taken, then sat down bedside me.

With the laser show in full swing below, the hostess who greeted me arrived with a second glass of champagne and a mini chocolate birthday cake with a lighted candle on top, 'with the compliments of the management'. I was choked by the gesture and tears welled up in my eyes.

'What's the celebration?' asked my new neighbour. I told her my story and we got into conversation. Her name was Natalie.

'Can I ask what brings you to be drinking here alone?' I asked, always curious.

Her husband was away on business, in Macau, but she didn't want to miss the laser show as they were returning to Paris in the morning.

'He's booked a table in the restaurant on the mezzanine. Have you eaten?'

I hadn't.

'I hate eating alone. Why don't you join me after the light show?'

Why not? I thought, and accepted her invitation.

The first thing Natalie did was order a bottle of Dom Perignon. Well, I nearly fainted! *Oh no... there goes all my spending money for five days in Hong Kong!* I thought. She must have noticed my face turn pale.

'Oh, Brigid, please don't worry. We'll put it on

my husband's account. We have to celebrate your birthday properly!'

I breathed a sigh of relief before enjoying a wonderful dinner with attentive service. I had a distinct impression, from the way the staff fawned, that she was a special regular customer.

As we were finishing up Natalie rang Danny, her chauffeur (as one does), to come and pick us up.

'I do hope you'll come up for a nightcap?' she asked. I have to finish packing for Paris but I'd love some company.' There was a hint that her life was not a total bed of roses.

I was highly unlikely to see inside the Peninsula Hotel any other way, so I replied with a firm 'yes please'!

There was Danny, the chauffeur, waiting downstairs in his peaked cap and holding open the door of a green Rolls Royce. He and Natalie seemed to be old friends, practically bosom pals. At the Peninsula we took a lift to her suite on the top floor – yes, a whole suite. Apparently, they had the same apartment whenever they were in Hong Kong; it comprised a corner of the building looking both south and west, and gave unmatchable views.

I stayed another half hour with her, looking out onto Hong Kong, chatting and sipping yet more champagne. She insisted that Danny drive me back to my hotel, so off I toddled in the Rolls. I still felt like Cinderella, leaving the ball without her glass slipper but quite laid-back compared to when I arrived. What a memorable evening, all thanks to the hostess taking pity on me and to meeting Natalie.

I returned to my room as happy as a pig in shit.

'Oo-ooh, you're the night owl, aren't you?' crooned Fred and Ruby, in unison, as I flung myself on the very ordinary bed. 'We thought you'd left us to fend for ourselves.'

'That'll never happen. You should know better,' I assured them, before recounting every last detail of my incredible evening.

I was more than ready for a good night's sleep, but I lay awake thinking about how such an unimaginable day had cut away at my qualms and apprehension. As I hugged the pillow, I hoped that my journey would not go downhill from this high point. My Michael would be very proud of me. *I can't wait to see what tomorrow brings!* I murmured, as I dropped off.

Chapter 6

JUMPING THE QUEUE

Last night had been like a fairy tale, and I awoke convinced for a moment that I had dreamed it. But no, I'd definitely had a wonderful day followed by an unforgettable celebration. Today, was Sunday, and having decided back home that no matter where I was on a Sunday I would attend Mass, I had already found the nearest Catholic church. The friendly receptionist directed me to the Gothic revival-style Cathedral of the Immaculate Conception, near the Mid-Levels Escalator, where English Mass was spoken at nine-thirty. The cathedral was rebuilt after a fire in 1888, then massively restored for the twenty-first century; it had vibrant stained-glass windows, a well-tuned choir, and I was surprised how many English-speaking families I was joining.

I was very keen to revisit the Peninsula Hotel

for high tea, so what better time than Sunday afternoon? I knew I might be disappointed, as I had no reservation, but I'm an optimist and, let's be fair, I was practically a regular, having sipped champagne in the penthouse only the previous night, and been driven home in the Rolls by Danny.

I turned up that afternoon to a long snaking line of people. *What are they doing? A wedding reception perhaps?* I soon found out that the winding hordes (yes, you've guessed) were all queuing for afternoon tea. *Shall I bother?* I thought. *Is it really worth it for a cake and scones?* I sneakily longed for Natalie to be there to put in a good word or use her influence but then rebuked myself: I would never jump the queue – would I?

I was about to give up and leave when, as fate had it, I tried to amuse the baby in front of me who was growing quite restless in its buggy. Would the child interact with me or scream its head off? It could have gone either way. I struck up a conversation; not only with the baby, but with the elegantly-dressed parents. The mother was asking all the usual sociable questions: where I was from and was it my first time in Hong Kong? They too were queuing for tea. However, *they* had a reservation.

The maître d'hôtel approached them: Did they

have a reservation? Yes, they did. And...? You've guessed again. They invited me to join them. How could I possibly refuse? It transpired that they were French; he was an investment banker and she was a lawyer; no common or garden couple for me. Oh, and their nanny was with them – and no, it wasn't me!

We spent a delightful time together. I thoroughly enjoyed the family company, and high tea was all that I expected.

Having been pleasantly spoiled, I set off for Evening Mass at Holy Cross Church. A thank you seemed in order for my wonderful stay in Hong Kong. The choir were all youngsters with poignant and sonorous voices that hung in the air.

Then I blessed a wedding in Kowloon Park... No, only kidding! But I did find ten men and women practicing Tai Chi in Kowloon.

One of them clocked me taking a spellbound interest in their fluid movements. She gave a big smile, stretched out her hand and pulled me into the group. Another complete stranger.

Oh, no, no, no,' complained Fred. 'You're really not wearing the right footwear. Have you lost your mind?'

I would put their ages at seventy years upwards.

Some might have been nearer to a hundred, but my over-riding impression of them all was of graceful strength and elegant agility.

By contrast, I felt like an out-of-control elephant. I was self-conscious and clumsy among these ultra slim men and women. To make it worse they were so very polite and patient in encouraging me to do the Tai Chi exercises with them. When the session was over, I felt privileged at having been included, even if Fred and I had made fools of ourselves. I thanked the group and scuttled off feeling a touch of embarrassment, but mostly humility. It was a salutary lesson about my limitations. I made a mental note: *Yes, I'll hone my Tai Chi skills as soon as I get home. Not right now – time's against me.* Well, that was my excuse anyway.

'I told you this would end in embarrassment – didn't I?' said Fred.

'Well, I thought we managed pretty well,' I retorted.

This propitious series of coincidences on the first stage of my journey filled me with excitement and confidence to keep going. My doubts and anxieties receded a little more each day as I recognised that I must have an angel on my shoulder in addition to those incorrigible travelling companions, Ruby and Fred, who were most definitely looking out for me.

Reflecting on my experiences of Hong Kong on this last day, I reminded myself that this was my very first venture to the Asian continent. It was so different to anywhere I had visited when playing golf in Europe and yet I had come to feel at ease, even safe going out at night. I was aware of a flowing relief that I had jumped high enough to negotiate my first hurdle.

What had happened to the vulnerable gibbering woman who stood like a rabbit frozen in the bright airport lights as she attempted to leave the Arrivals' Hall only a week ago? That woman was completely out of her comfort zone and within a hair's breadth of getting back on the plane and returning to the safety of her little house in Brighton! Where had she disappeared to? Well, she survived it, but I knew she could not fall into the trap of feeling complacent or cocky. There would be plenty of new obstacles.

Would you want to come back here? I asked myself. *Yes, in a flash!* After the spontaneous generosity of the people I met, which broke the ice and allayed my worst fears about travelling alone, I loved my time in Hong Kong. Indeed, had I been travelling with someone, I probably would not have engaged with local people, whereas on my own I had to pluck up courage and ask for help when I was lost for what to do next. The rewards were beyond my wildest hopes, and I was repeatedly stunned by the kindness of strangers.

'It's not easy!', Michael used to tell me, especially if I was pestering him to do a job around the house. I imagined him watching me make my intrepid way through these new experiences, parrying against the butterflies inside me, and he'd be delighted to see my progress.

Chapter 7

NO BED OF ROSES

So, what can I tell you about Michael? His charms and quirks. His good times and bad. We met on a Sunday night at an Irish dance hall in London. My boyfriend was working in Manchester, so I wasn't too bothered about dancing, but I towed along to keep my friend Joan company. Joan had a fiancé in Ireland who she was committed to through an arranged marriage. Yes, they still existed. Joan spotted Michael first, and she really fancied him.

I was dancing in The Siege of Ennis, a fast, traditional set dance where eight boys faced eight girls and everyone moved down the line. I found myself facing Munro who had an untidy mop of ginger hair and was infamous for his wild ways. *Oh hell!* He was notorious for swinging the girls much too fast. Suddenly, for a laugh, he let me go, and there I was sliding across the polished wood floor on my bum only to land in a messy heap at Michael's feet!

'Aha! I've never had a girl throw herself at my feet begging me to dance,' he chuckled. For a while I was utterly mortified, but within minutes my chap in Manchester had become history!

Michael's downside stemmed from the fact that Irishmen and drink travel hand in hand. Being naïve throughout our courtship, I reckoned the love of a good woman (me) could change him. But, of course, it doesn't work like that.

After our marriage, Michael – who liked a pint or three – fell in with a new set of drinking buddies. He was always first up to the bar buying the round, so he was very popular too. When everyone was well tanked up, he would invite these so-called friends back to our house where I was expected to feed them.

This went on for quite some time. I hated the sight of these leeches coming through the door and they knew it, but, full of Dutch courage, they revelled in the idea that I carried on serving them where the barmaid left off. Finally, I'd had enough, and imagined I could fix the problem by moving house:

far away from these cronies, Michael might stop drinking.

So, we moved., but I didn't get a result. *Maybe if we have another child*, I thought, changing strategy. So, I had two daughters in quick succession, but that didn't work either. When he was sober you could not meet a nicer man, which was why I stayed. I kept clutching at straws, one after the other. *Maybe it's okay to just like a drink*, I would tell myself. *One day he'll stop drinking... for me.*

We were always invited to parties because Michael was the life and soul of them. Everybody loved him, and I was left looking like a miserable old bag. Even today I can hear people say, 'Why don't you leave him alone, Brigid? He's only having a bit of fun!' as he danced on a table. I often left early and alone because I felt ashamed, miserable, and so, so uncomfortable. His drinking got worse as the night went on. In the end I began to believe that I was a spoilsport and it must somehow be my fault. After all, he would not drink so much if he was happily married.

Life went from bad to worse over the years, until he would go straight to the pub after work and only come home when they threw him out. I spent my young life worried sick that he would lose his job.

What if he has a car accident on the way home? When are we going to be out on the street because we can't pay the bills? Things became dreadful in our marriage once alcoholism had reared its ruinous head and wormed its way into every part of our family life. I needed a backup plan.

I had to get a job of some kind. I couldn't work in the daytime as my girls were pre school-age, and my son was not old enough to look after them. Carol, who lived a few doors down the street, suggested working nights in a nursing home. I could work from 9 p.m. until 7 a.m. on Fridays and Saturdays.

She said the children could stay with her until Michael got back from the pub, or even sleep at her house so I could pick them up after breakfast. It worked, and I started at the nursing home two nights a week, which lifted some pressure and worry from my shoulders. Not only did it help pay the bills – it gave me a lifeline. When I look back to that unhappy time, it seems like someone else's life. Desperate times meant desperate measures, and Carol's generosity was a lifesaver. I don't know how we'd have survived them without her help.

As for my mother, God rest her soul, she never helped me. She followed in the footsteps of her own mother – cold, callous, unforgiving, cruel, lacking empathy – and was matriarchal in her demeanour. She ruled our household with an iron rod. I never told her about the extent of Michael's drinking and the impact it was having on my life. She would have written him off as a weak man who was easily led.

Back in Ireland when a child was confirmed it was customary for them to take The Pledge and wear a Pioneer Pin as part of the Pioneer Total Abstinence Association, because alcoholism was endemic among Irish Catholics. Having taken this pledge meant to my mother that she would refrain from alcohol for the rest of her life – which she did.

Once, at the end of my tether, when I contemplated sleeping in a park with the children, if need be, I asked my mother if I could move back home, just until I got on my feet.

'No, Brigid, you can't,' she told me. 'You've made your bed and now you can lie in it.'

I have never forgotten her words. When Mother died, I did not shed a single tear. I had grown totally detached. I felt nothing. I might have allowed that bad relationship with my mother to destroy my life.

The only positive quality my mother passed on to me was the strength to survive, and maybe her unsympathetic words that day were the reason I did.

Chapter 8

THE MEN FROM AA

Is this really it? For the rest of my life? I was staring out of my kitchen window in despair. I knew I had to take action, but I had no idea what. As we reached our lowest point, I had a brain wave; a sudden memory of where to turn. I rummaged through the phone book for Alcoholics Anonymous and got through. They listened to me attentively and asked when would be the best time to come and meet Michael?

'Sunday,' I told them. 'He doesn't go to the pub on Sundays.'

My mind did somersaults: they might take him away... or send him to hospital... my nightmare would be over. I even fantasised about getting a night's sleep. Sunday couldn't come around fast enough; I was bubbling with expectation that the AA experts were coming to sort out my problems.

When I told Michael that people were coming on Sunday to help him with his drinking problem, he laughed at me.

'Why? I'm not an alcoholic!'

'We'd like to speak to Michael on his own, please,' declared the visitors. So, I went into the dining room. When they had spoken to him, they came to report back to me.

'I'm afraid we can't help your husband...'

My hopes were cruelly dashed. I was dumbfounded and distraught.

'...but we can help you,' the man added. '*You* can come along to an Al-Anon meeting.'

'Al-Anon? What's that?' I asked in astonishment. 'It's my husband needs help, not me.... I'm not the alcoholic here!'

'Until Michael admits that he's an alcoholic and *asks* for our help, I'm afraid we can't do anything,' he went on. This first step is the most important: Michael has to admit he has a drink problem.'

'Well, that's never going to happen,' I told them. 'He says he just likes a drink.'

I felt the ground was crumbling under me.

'But Al-Anon is there...' said the first man, who had seen my crestfallen face, '...to support families like you, affected by living with an alcoholic.'

He looked up the nearest Al-Anon meeting and wrote down the details so I could attend it. I was unbelievably angry and felt as if I was being kicked in the teeth.

What a waste of time! I thought. *It's not me that needs help!* But having set the ball in motion, what could I lose?

'...Okay,' I gave in. 'I'm desperate enough to try anything.'

So, out of curiosity, I steeled myself to try this Al-Anon meeting on Tuesday, and see what it was about. My treasured neighbour, Carol, agreed to babysit as Michael quickly proclaimed that he would not be looking after the children.

'Not while you spend the evening swapping stories about drunken husbands!'

That first evening, I arrived in trepidation and trembling with nerves. I was knocked back by the sound of laughter as I walked in and assumed I was in the wrong room for Al-Anon. *These people can't possibly have the same problems as me. They're too cheerful!* I soon discovered that many of them had much worse problems.

My first takeaway from that room was that I was

not to blame. I had not caused my husband to be an alcoholic. It was not my fault. Next, I learned about the three Cs: I did not Cause it, I can't Control it, and I can't Cure it. I had wasted all those years thinking that I could stop Michael's drinking habit.

My heart melted with relief on hearing those statements, and realised that I was powerless over the alcoholism. The only things I was responsible for, they said, were my own actions and looking out for my children. I had to let go of Michael, take a good look at myself, and concentrate on making my own life better. I remember being extremely indignant when I was asked to consider my own shortcomings. *What shortcomings?* I thought. *It's not me that has the drink problem... it's him!* How naïve was I? This was a bitter pill to swallow, but I learned that until I dealt with my own faults, I would find no peace. Al-Anon offered me a parallel twelve step programme; the same twelve steps followed by alcoholics in their AA groups. As I had tried everything else that I could think of, and nothing had worked, I chose to give it a chance.

I joined Al-Anon meetings every Tuesday for nine months. I sat, listened, and tried as many suggestions as I could. The hardest part was still admitting my own faults and accepting that I was not perfect either. Those evenings encouraged me to 'detach with love' – now there was a paradox to get my head around. I was told to keep reaffirming those three C's: I didn't Cause it – I can't Control it – I can't Cure it. "Detaching" did not mean I should abandon Michael or stop caring about him. He could still be a wonderful human being and, luckily, was never violent towards me or the children. Nor was he ever absent from work. But now I knew I could *not* stop him drinking. He had to reach that conclusion by himself. If I left him alone, he would fall asleep in the chair after a drinking session. Deep down I recognised a hope that my new "education" might trigger a change in him and, by some miracle, he would seek help by attending an AA meeting.

One Tuesday evening I was in the kitchen preparing the children's supper when the back door opened and there stood their father – sober at five-thirty. I felt as if I was seeing a ghost. *Why's he come home?* I thought. *He must be ill...*

Usually, Michael came back at closing time when the landlord ordered him to leave, so this was a first. His eyes were as clear as could be and I absolutely knew he was sober. His eyes always told the tale about his drinking.

'Brigid,' he said. 'I want to go to an AA meeting. Will you come with me?'

I thought I had misheard. You could have knocked me down with a feather.

'What's brought this on?' I asked.

'I just want some of what you've got, Brigid.'

'What do you mean?'

'You've changed. You treat me like a human being. You're never sarcastic anymore. You've shown me so much kindness... for the first time in years.'

I felt guilty. He brought home to me what an uncaring cow I had become. At last, for the first time, I broke down and cried my eyes dry. All those years of anger, bitterness and resentment seemed to dissolve and melt away. You see, the difference was that now I understood that alcoholism was a *disease*, and Michael was powerless over it. He was not evil, or any of the other names I'd used. He just needed help... and compassion.

Up to that evening, his regular comment when I came home from Al-Anon was, 'Well, have you been with your *roast-the-alcoholic* friends?' I always repeated that I had enough to do sorting myself out and didn't have time to vilify an alcoholic.

'Yes, Michael,' I said, when my tears allowed me. 'I'll come to an AA meeting with you tonight.' I did not remind him that Tuesdays were my own meeting nights. I knew this could be life changing for all of us, and hopefully herald a new life for him.

He had done his homework, and found an open meeting not far away, which meant that non-alcoholics could also attend. This was my first AA meeting too and, in my ignorance, I expected the participants to be down-and-outs who lived in cardboard boxes under the railway arches. Michael had been through hell, and it was eleven years before he attended this first AA meeting. With only one short interlude, when after nine dry months he felt safe to share a social drink, he continued attending AA for the rest of his life.

At the top table on this first evening sat the guest speakers: an airline pilot, an accountant, a doctor and a clergyman. I am rarely lost for words (I was not allowed to speak here anyway) but I was dumbstruck when I found out that they were such pillars of society.

With a measure of sobriety under his belt, Michael spent a great deal of his time giving back service and helping others to deal with their alcoholism. It did not matter what time of day or night, which day of the week; if he had a distress call from a suffering alcoholic, he would spend hours getting them through their crisis. He never forgot the help he was given when he was first struggling to stay sober.

I will always be grateful to AA and Al-Anon for giving us back our lives. When he found an AA meeting in Croydon, Michael became a regular attender. Al-Anon and Alateen were situated in the same building, so it made sense for me, and both my daughters, to go to our respective support groups in the same place. Our son did not wish to attend.

Patrick had been in AA for quite a few years, and became Michael's sponsor. His wife Philomena attended Al-Anon and also ran the Alateen youth group.

After one Thursday meeting, Patrick invited us back for coffee, and we discovered that he, Philomena and their five children lived over an off-licence. He was area manager, while Philomena managed the off-licence. It seemed absurd that their invited AA and Al-Anon guests were sitting right above thousands of bottles of beer, wine and spirits, but we soon found out how people in the pub and hospitality trade often find themselves confronted with major drinking challenges. It's well documented. After all, they work long hours with permanent temptation in front of them.

We attended the Irish AA Convention for a number of years. It took place for one week during the summer months and at the end of the convention we all headed off – in convoy – to Donegal for a holiday. Once, Michael, Catherine and I were asked to be speakers at the convention's closing meeting. By then, Catherine and Siobhan were active members of Alateen. We shared our experiences and how this fellowship had helped us handle our lives, one day at a time. It was an unforgettable occasion for each of us in different ways.

One year, with Patrick and Philomena, we attended the AA World Convention in San Diego, California. Had drinking continued to rule our lives, we would have been lucky to have a roof over our heads, much less go to California! How things had changed. I gained so much insight by digging up enough courage to attend that first Al-Anon meeting. We were now living in a sober household, one day at a time; it was an idyllic period of our lives.

But every now and then, vivid memories flash into my mind, enough to make me appreciate how far we travelled. One Saturday night, now in the distant past, Michael came home blind drunk with his friend Kenneth in tow. Although this fellow weighed about twenty stone, I only had a sun lounger for him to sleep on. We found him on the floor, next morning, still on the sun lounger, which had collapsed under his weight into a mangled wreck only fit for the dustbin. Despite the situation, I couldn't stop laughing at him snoring on the floor, and occasionally I wondered whether he ever became sober.

Well, the next and last time I saw him, he put his hand on mine and squeezed it in sympathy. I was standing in the front pew at Michael's funeral. I looked up and there was Ken almost thirty years since the sun lounger episode. I had never given a thought to how he respected Michael or how loyal he was, but he had heard of Michael's death and come down from Peckham to be there for me. The world is certainly full of surprises, and this was one of those humbling times.

I was blown away at the people who had travelled from all over the UK and other countries to pay tribute to him. The church was overflowing and many friends had to stand outside in the grounds. It was an emotional day for us all but for Michael's ninety-one-year-old mother it was especially heartbreaking to be at her son's funeral. The whole family visit her in Croydon up to this day, and she is still going strong at a young 109 years old.

Chapter 9

EXTRAS, MADAM?

Carrying the heartache of missing Michael, I found myself in the airport lounge, waiting for my flight to Thailand. I could not shake Hong Kong from my thoughts, nor believe that I was moving on seamlessly to Bangkok from a city that had exceeded every expectation on so many levels, like its central escalator system. Hong Kong was my first faltering step into unknown territory and, as such, the exhilaration and freedom it bestowed on me will always hold a special place in my heart. Some of my escapades, like climbing up to the Big Buddha and, far worse, struggling down backwards, still make me shudder. I know Fred was impressed with my courage because he said as much, but Ruby was particularly relieved.

'You do realise I could have tumbled right down all those steps and been ripped to shreds, don't you?

Thank Buddha you left me at home!'

I deserved a metaphoric pat on the back for being brave, even at my most vulnerable. It had turned out to be a good place to dip my toes into the water and, being now armed with a measure of confidence, I couldn't wait to explore Bangkok.

But pride comes before a fall. To my surprise, Hong Kong had in no way prepared me for Bangkok.

I arrived with a spring in my step and full of excited anticipation, but it was excruciatingly noisy and chaotic compared to the order I had left behind. I was becoming a bit of an expert lepidopterist by now, as those butterflies returned bringing fear and panic with a vengeance. The temporary successes of Hong Kong had lulled me into a false sense of security, but here I was faced with chaos and confusion again. If Bangkok had been my initial destination, I'm pretty sure I'd have turned on my heels with the culture shock.

'Calm yourself down Brigid!' Ruby firmly reminded me. 'You know the score – it's one step at a time.'

Nothing could have been more unlike my sedate existence at home, and fears I thought I'd banished flooded back. I couldn't vouch for my ability to cope with Bangkok. But, this time, I kept going.

Massive signs everywhere I looked, bore red crosses and warnings about not bringing fruit into the country. *Is it really a serious offence?* A woman in front of me had forgotten an innocent apple in her hand luggage... until the sniffer dogs unearthed it. Customs' police arrived from nowhere and forcibly escorted her to their offices. I put myself in her shoes: *She must be terrified. That could be me being whisked off and grilled. What an awful start to Thailand!* Thank God I had no fresh produce on me.

Out in the stifling warm air, I was faced with a barrage of drivers all touting for my business, 'Ride, lady? Ride?' I gulped and took a step back. Help.

'Where the hell are you taking us now?' grumbled Ruby. 'I didn't sign up for this! You know I hate being jostled.'

Irrational storylines flitted through my head about getting into a taxi and never being seen again. I looked around for guidance. I needed help.

'Hey, look over there!' said Ruby. 'How about that handsome man in uniform...'

Thankfully the handsome man spoke English and explained that his stand offered fixed-price taxis that were licensed to trade at the airport. He could supply a regular taxi, or a limousine if I preferred, and called to one of his *bona fide* drivers. I paid his requested fare to the hotel that Grainne had pre-booked, and he issued a receipt. It felt considerably more manageable.

The traffic was horrendous. *Thank God I'm not driving.* I thought. *I'll never ever complain about London traffic again.* I asked the driver if the traffic was always like this.

'No, lady, this is a good day,' he informed me, and he went on to offer his favourite tips for visits off the tourist beat.

I settled on the bed with aching muscles and frayed nerves and decided on a short nap before dinner. This hotel was central and safe, and I felt my body relaxing. I had a good feeling about it. *Relax*, the word got me thinking... *Thai massage?* Did I feel brave enough? *Steady on!* I thought. *Don't get ahead of yourself.* I dozed off remembering that following my gut feeling about people and places was my new guiding mantra!

With that firmly in mind, I set off to ferret out a restaurant rather than sticking with dinner in the hotel. My resolution was rewarded by a small family restaurant that served genuine Thai cooking. I had genned up on hello and goodbye in Thai, but was greeted in English by a smiling young woman who sat me down and offered me the menu – in Thai of course!

The only dish I recognised was *chow mein* and, as I fancied something familiar, *chow mein* it was to be. Luckily it was delicious. The family made me really welcome, and I was introduced to authentic Thai flavours.

I still had plenty of time to slot in a massage. Nikki, my childhood friend Ellie's daughter, had been to Thailand many times and enjoyed taking in the culture. She recommended an excellent massage place that was quite close by.

'I'm off to pamper myself after that journey. Please behave yourself, Ruby.'

'And you be careful! I've heard what those massage parlours are like!'

I ignored her (she gets above herself sometimes) and carefully followed Nikki's directions to the massage salon. After a quick glance at the building, I was less sure about venturing inside. *Have I got the right place?* I wondered. *Did Nikki really mean this?* The tiny shop front and plain wooden door were far from luxurious; they were pretty ramshackle in fact. I stepped inside self-consciously and was shown into a waiting room; nervous, but with just an inkling of trust that things might work out okay. *What have I got to lose?* I asked myself. After all, Nikki had vouched for it, so nothing could possibly go wrong, could it?

I sat patiently, observing how a number of men came in and went straight upstairs. A European chap sat opposite me looking sheepish and avoiding eye contact. I think he was wishing me to disappear. He clearly was not there for the beer, and was eventually escorted upstairs by two women, and stared resolutely ahead as he passed me. I imagine he was there for the 'special' treatments.

An older woman, probably the owner, came over and spoke to me in good English (definitely more satisfactory than my non-existent Thai). She liked hearing that her parlour had been recommended by my friend who had always been happy with her treatments, and it won me a warm smile of welcome. Two slight young women ushered me to the massage area, and I looked forward to them gently cosseting me for at least an hour.

But aren't looks deceiving? These delicate girls looked as if they would fall over if you blew on them. But they were wolves in sheep's clothing! No chance of the indulgent coddling that I longed for. My images of luxuriating in a little piece of heaven and floating on clouds were fast dispelled as those two demure, smiling, pretty young things spent an extremely long hour pummelling, kneading, and deliberately torturing me. At times, I couldn't choose between wallowing in ecstasy or crying out in pain. How had I been sucked into this notion that a soothing massage would be just the job after my flight? I planned to do some serious sightseeing in the morning, and now I was wondering if I'd even be able to get out of bed.

The session became a roller coaster ride: I was swerving between being lulled into meditative calm and then finding myself in a torture chamber! The masseuses found every knot in every muscle and every build-up of calcium behind my shoulders. One moment I wanted to weep with pain and, next, I wanted to fall asleep in euphoria. If you have had a Thai massage, you will be wiser than I was and know that its practitioners don't take prisoners; the process swings between heaven and sheer hell.

But, like with so many challenging experiences, I have often wished myself back in that Thai massage parlour. The 'no pain, no gain' maxim is particularly apposite, because after those girls had finished with me, and I had paid a ridiculously small amount for my treatment, I veritably floated back to the hotel.

On my way, I called at the tourist office to find a day trip that would break me in gently until I acclimatised to the hustle and bustle of Bangkok street-life. They suggested the Summer Palace as an iconic place to start, so that was me sorted for tomorrow.

I glided into the hotel on my first evening in Thailand having had quite a day of it. Ruby was fast asleep, bundled on top of Fred in the corner, and I was beyond exhausted. The next thing I remember was the alarm buzzing me awake at 6 a.m.

Chapter 10

IS THIS THE *REAL* THAILAND?

After a standard fare Western breakfast of toast and cereals I was outside by seven. I had little idea what to expect from the Summer Palace and return trip on the Chao Phraya River, but I was eager to embrace whatever lay in store.

My American travelling companions, were already aboard the mini-bus when I arrived. They were in Bangkok for a wedding later in the week, and keen to introduce themselves to an Irishwoman with a Kilkenny accent.

Andy, the groom, was on board with his best-man from back home. It was everyone else's first time in Thailand, so we were all in the same boat, or mini-bus, with no one knowing what to expect, apart from Andy who wanted to offer them a flavour of Thailand.

We headed north through Bangkok in

air-conditioned luxury until an hour later we reached Bang Pa-in, the Summer Palace, an entire complex used by Thai royalty since the seventeenth century.

The day flowed in absolute peace until we were transported from the sublime to the ridiculous on the Chao Phraya River Bus for our return journey. As the first people on board, it felt roomy and comfortable: we almost had the boat to ourselves and I blithely imagined we might even be served drinks. But I was soon disillusioned when it stopped regularly along the river picking up more and more punters and became so crowded, I worried that it might sink (I am not a good swimmer). We made it back, pressed in with milling passengers, but dry, to a mini-bus in Bangkok city where we saw immediately that the traffic was in complete gridlock.

Lucky for us, Andy had lived in Bangkok for twelve years and knew his way around.

'Quit the bus! It's not leaving anytime soon,' he said. 'Come on... we'll get back before it.'

He guided us through the amassed tuk-tuks, down side roads, winding along nooks and crannies until, lo and behold, there was the hotel! Left alone, I would still be wandering around Bangkok like a headless chicken!

Adrenaline levels were still high as I swept into

my room, only to find a very dejected rucksack.

'What's wrong with me?' complained Ruby. 'How come I don't get to go out to palaces with you guys?'

'Good point,' said Fred, without subtlety. 'You missed a royal day!'

'You know what? I'm not happy being useless and abandoned,' she scolded.

'Sorry Ruby, my bad,' I said. 'Come with us tomorrow... really, you'll be helpful.'

I was acclimatising to the noise of Bangkok. *Are most capital cities like this?* The fluttering of wings inside was definitely growing gentler as my confidence grew, and maybe the butterflies' antennae were helping to guide me through the hubbub.

I pondered how to pass the evening. *Dinner!* I reminded myself sternly. I easily get carried away when I'm engrossed in new places and forget to eat until I become ravenous and would try anything!

Bangkok street vendors are renowned for the huge variety of tempting fresh food. I fancied an authentic stir-fry and was drawn by smells wafting from a stall where, quick as a flash, an array of colourful local vegetables and spices were chopped, mixed, and tossed in a massive wok by expert hands right in front of me. Those aromas were mouth-watering, and watching the vendor putting together herbs and veggies I had never seen before, and in this bustling street atmosphere, was a joy. I fell in love with Thai food there and then, and still enjoy it at home when it's done well.

So, with growing confidence next morning, I grabbed Ruby as promised and skipped the hotel breakfast in favour of a quirky eating place right across the street. It was an outdoor diner with a long counter around a covered cooking area. The customers perched on bar stools calling out their orders to kitchen assistants who passed them on to the cooks who prepared everything from scratch while you waited. At 50 Thai baht for a full cooked breakfast, it was a bargain and my courage felt well repaid.

I found myself sitting beside an American and asked him if the food was good. Apparently, he always came here for breakfast when he was in Bangkok and had never been disappointed. *If it's good enough for him*, I thought, *I'm probably onto a winner*. So, while breakfast was on the hob, we chatted away. No, I don't seek out Americans! It was pure coincidence meeting them two days running. There must have been a lot of them about.

'You do know this isn't the *real* Thailand, don't you?' he proclaimed with a streak of arrogance.

I was shocked and disappointed at him starting the conversation with one-upmanship. *Here we go – another weirdo. What a positive start to my day.* And I wished I had not sat next to the miserable old devil.

I gave him the benefit of the doubt, though, and awaited his explanation. It turned out that he had spent eleven years in Thailand over a thirty-year career photographing for the *National Geographic*.

'Next time you visit Thailand, don't stop here,' he went on. 'Take a taxi to the internal airport and fly to Chiang Mai. That's *real* Thailand. Tour the southern islands.'

These are the little gems one learns when travelling alone, but I had to take his word for it and put them on a bucket list for another time.

'Well, that was a bit of a downer,' said Ruby. 'But did you notice... he was quite dishy!'

'I knew you'd be helpful,' I answered.

Feeling replete, I stood on the pavement figuring out the best route to the Grand Palace, home of the Thai royal family, when an old lady noticed my confusion and indicated she might be able to help. I showed her the palace photos and she beckoned me towards a ticket office, where she explained to the clerk and I paid him. The ticket informed me, in

English and Thai, that I could travel to the Grand Palace by Skytrain and return by boat. I knew nothing about a Skytrain in Bangkok, nor, importantly, where to find it. But the woman did not leave me at the ticket desk. She led me up the escalator, onto the platform, and stayed next to me, smiling all the time until the train arrived and the door opened to reveal passengers packed tight like sardines. She singled out a woman near the door and I could tell by her body language that this passenger was delegated to make sure I got off at the right stop. I had bumped into the right person because this woman, who was probably in her late eighties, did not take prisoners; she was terrier-like on my behalf and the passenger in charge of me carried out her instructions as if her life depended on it.

I had never seen a Skytrain, much less travelled on one. It travelled speedily, high above the bustling streets so I was looking onto the buildings below. Because traffic in Bangkok is so horrendously congested, the Skytrain was my best option to move quickly around the city and avoid pollution. I saw eyebrow-raising skywalks leading off the Skytrain platforms to shopping malls. Having discovered that such things existed, I resolved to pop them on this morning's bucket list and visit the malls 'next time'.

I stopped counting how many stations we passed and was wondering if my guardian actually knew where to put me off but, as we pulled into the next station, she gesticulated that it was my stop.

'Here! Here! Here! You get off here,' she shouted, waving her arm to the left of the platform. 'And no go with tuk-tuks!' she added.

Now, that's what I call service. I was becoming a solid believer in the kindness of strangers, and have not been disappointed – yet!

'Bit frantic, isn't she?' said Ruby.

As I walked through the white walls of the Grand Palace compound, I noticed that officials were enforcing a modesty dress code. Arms and legs had to be covered and no open-toed shoes were permitted. A demure Australian in front of me was turned away because she wore sandals with open fronts.

'Lucky I'm here, or you'd be chucked out for not conforming to regulations,' pointed out Fred.

'You've made your point, Fred. You can stay,' I agreed.

The Reclining Buddha at Wat Pho, was inspiring to behold. At 46m long and 15m high, it dwarfed me. I was also completely mesmerized by the beauty of the Grand Palace and Wat Arun, the Temple of Dawn (especially stunning at first light).

My last day in Bangkok had arrived and I couldn't fathom where the time had gone? But I could not leave without visiting the Holy Rosary Catholic Church, built by the Portuguese colonists back in 1786, on the banks of the Chao Phraya River.

As I approached the church, four students stopped me with a carefully-ordered set of questions and introduced themselves as Sam, Gard, Eustace and Paul.

'May we ask... where are you from, madam?'

I told them.

'Have you been to Bangkok before?'

'Are you a Catholic?'

Once I had satisfied their interest, they offered to show me around the beautiful cloistered environment that offers respite from the city's pace. I was delighted, especially as they were from the local congregation, and two of them sang in the choir. They must have been considered very trustworthy because they even had a set of keys and gave me a comprehensive tour, including areas not normally open to the public. I felt moved and privileged by this gesture. They were all studying architecture at the university, so had some interesting insights into the building.

After we had finished my private tour of the church, they asked if I would join them at one of their favourite eating places. I was thrilled to, especially as they could explain the different dishes and make suggestions. I fancied traditional food, but not too spicy, and asked them to surprise me; so, that evening I had a whole new Thai foodie experience. They offered me a guided tour of their city next day but, sadly, I was flying to Singapore in the morning. I was delighted with their open-hearted and welcoming company, and we exchanged email addresses. I have returned to Bangkok since, and still meet up with Gard and his friends.

Despite my initial alarm at the city's hurly-burly, I was leaving with a touch of sadness. There and then I vowed to return one day and see Chiang Mai in the north and those 'real' southern islands, just to satisfy my curiosity about what the National Geographic photographer was so enamoured with.

Chapter 11

LUCK OF THE DRAW

Once again at Suvarnabhumi airport, I found myself in front of a cheerful check-in clerk from Cathay Pacific, who behaved impeccably even though I felt self-conscious, like an eccentric granny trying to relive her youth with Fred and Ruby as backpacking chums.

She handed over my boarding pass, which clearly proclaimed FIRST CLASS. Spotting my reaction, and before I could open my mouth, she nodded that she had upgraded me and wished me a wonderful flight. I realised she wanted to be subtle, as others behind me were unlikely to receive this privilege, and I obligingly moved on.

But I was gobsmacked and couldn't believe my luck. I felt a sudden rush of emotion and unfairness that Michael was not by my side to enjoy it too. Travel seemed all swings and roundabouts, and this flight balanced out my less pleasant London experience. I couldn't help wishing, avariciously, that this was a long-haul journey – maybe to New Zealand or some other far-flung place!

'It's a first for me, in both senses, Ruby.'

'Yeah… me too!' she answered, with enthusiasm. 'Let's get on board before the others!'

'A little dignity please,' I reminded her.

I strolled nonchalantly into the first-class lounge.

'Classy carpet,' pointed out Fred.

I imagined wry glances from fellow travellers at my boots on the plush.

People were leaving the lounge and I went to check my watch. *Have I missed an announcement? Why no call yet? It's nearly time for departure.*

'Please don't worry, madam. First-class passengers will board the plane last, through a different entrance. We haven't forgotten you.'

And within moments a flight attendant was taking Ruby from my hand without blinking an eye, as if she were a Louis Vuitton suitcase.

With only one seat either side of the aisle, it felt like my own private jet. *Hey, Siobhan and Catherine, eat your hearts out! Look at your mother – a First Class high-flyer!*

Across the aisle in seat 1B sat a business woman

who spent the flight working on her laptop. The attendant arrived to offer me champagne. No, she was not balancing a tray of pre-poured glasses; she presented a wine list for me to choose from a selection of champagnes! I hadn't a clue which to pick, but her recommendation came up trumps – simply heavenly.

I was now mellow and perusing a menu and wine list that would put many five-star restaurants to shame. I was so spoiled for choice that I did not know where to begin. My stewardess was fantastic. Yes, she felt like *my* stewardess because she was only serving one other passenger. Having ordered dinner, I rested back in my seat and mused about Michael not being here to share this fun. I am missing my other friends too.

I had met Nikki (remember the Thai massage parlour?) through her mother, Ellie, a childhood friend who became my closest saviour and support in those days before Alcoholics Anonymous entered our life.

Like Michael, Ellie's husband Jack had problems with alcohol. We used to commiserate about our difficult lives, always supported each other, and have never lost touch. Nikki had recently invited me to celebrate Ellie's birthday and I was delighted to see that she and her siblings have grown up into fine people despite their difficult childhood. It came out, as we chatted all those years later, that her married life had been much worse than mine. Jack, it seems, was a gambler, wife-beater, and spent any infrequent wages in the betting shop or pub. He would come home drunk and demand the money she had earned to maintain herself and the children. When she refused on one occasion, he picked up a hot plate of food from the supper table and threw it at her. Their teenage son, Jack Junior, witnessed this and manhandled his father out of the house. When his father kept banging to come back in, the boy opened the door, and knocked him out cold on the pavement with a resonant 'Fuck off!'. That was the last time Ellie laid eyes on her husband. Years later poor Nikki found him sleeping under the arches in London. She tried to help him then, but he was not interested, and shortly after their meeting he was found dead while still living rough.

Ellie's family and ours started out with similar heartaches, but Jack never got sober and their world fell apart. Fate had it that my children and I had a different experience. We were the lucky ones. Michael never laid a finger on me, and always held down a job in spite of his drinking. When he eventually found sobriety, he spent the rest of his life paying back the help he received by supporting other suffering alcoholics.

The plight of women and families receives more attention nowadays, with provision of safe havens for victims of abuse due to alcohol or drug addictions, but it's not enough. So much goes on behind closed doors. I still have friends who I met all those years ago at Al-Anon meetings, and they know they can call on me day or night if they need help.

Dinner arrived, and with it appeared the captain.

'Just checking that you're comfortable and happy with our service today?'

'Absolutely,' I told him, 'But I do have a small favour. Could you possibly fly me first class to Brisbane when I've finished with Singapore?'

'Sorry madam. I'd love to… but we don't fly to Brisbane.'

Well, I thought there was no harm in asking; it seemed worth a try.

Full of good food and wine, I rummaged in my complimentary travel bag very quietly so as not to make Ruby jealous or out of sorts. It contained the expected toothbrush, toothpaste and moisture cream, but how low my expectations proved when I found pyjamas, dressing gown, slippers, toiletries; the whole works. I was offered towels and all the accessories If I wanted to shower. *A shower on board?* I was open-eyed with astonishment. *What about someone to wash my back and knead my shoulders?* I didn't push my luck in case I woke up to find it was a dream.

I took an hour's sleep in my fully-reclining bed, and before I knew it we had touched down in Singapore.

Chapter 12

HIGH FLYER

It was at lunch with my fellow retired teachers, after Michael passed away, that I was telling them of my plan to travel around the world on my own. It provoked a barrage of questions.

'You're not serious?'

'You're not cracking up, are you?'

'Aren't you worried something will happen to you?'

I got the distinct impression they thought I was emotionally unbalanced.

'I've been invited to my friend Brenda's birthday celebration in Australia.' I told them.

The table fell silent.

'You are brave to go all that way on your own!' Someone broke the silence.

'Maybe I need to be brave... to start a new life...' That clearly made them think. 'I'm lucky to be healthy... have masses of energy... and I try to keep my glass always half full.

'I miss Michael, of course I do,' I confided. 'Especially getting into a cold bed with no one to say goodnight to or get a cuddle from.'

Was I over-sharing? Obviously, I'd have been happier to have Michael along with me, but that's not how things turned out.

'So, where are you going then?' clamoured different voices.

I explained how I'd come to buy a round-the-world ticket and where I'd chosen to see along the way. Pat offered to contact her son David.

'Siew Sai is David's business colleague. He lives in Singapore; maybe he could speak to him and ask him to show you around?'

Then Myfanwy butted in.

'Such a coincidence! I'll be in Sydney for Christmas and the New Year with my boy, Simon. Maybe we could be out there at the same time? We could meet up!'

I promised to be in Sydney for Christmas.

It felt great to already be building in some social structure and making appointments with friends. We gave each other a big hug to seal the promise.

Now that day had materialised, and here I was

in a Singapore taxi to the Rendezvous Hotel, a restored colonial building in the arts district. Like the Kowloon in Hong Kong and the Amari Boulevard in Bangkok, the celebrated Grainne had booked the Rendezvous from Brighton. My trusty travel agent; it seemed ages ago since I sat at her desk looking more like a drowned rat than a prospective customer. I remembered feeling timid as a mouse, praying she would not laugh at my hair-brained idea of travelling the world. And Grainne did not dismiss me but was pivotal in booking bases from where I could venture out bravely and feel confident. She realised that I could not have language barriers or get lost before I began exploring. She was right, and it certainly relieved me of pressure knowing I had a safe haven to relax in at the end of each day. Even though Singapore felt more European than the previous cities, there are times when it pays to be sensible. Michael did have a business friend who lived in Singapore, but I decided not to contact him – that's another story. Let's just say his agenda would have been very different from mine! But I recalled him saying that Singapore was spotlessly clean, and no chewing gum was permitted... anywhere. We had laughed and dismissed it as joking, but the first question addressed to me at customs was, 'Madam do you have chewing gum in your possession?' I'd had no idea it was actually a crime, but at least I could walk around the city without a lump of gum stuck to the sole of my shoe.

'Lucky you don't like chewing gum!' piped up Ruby. I poked her discreetly, so the customs officer didn't ask questions about her. Meanwhile, Fred considered himself special to be legally protected from chewing gum gunging up his treads.

What if the hotel clerk speaks in Mandarin... or Malay... or Tamil? I'll be in a right fix! I wondered, but I soon realised that I need not worry. The receptionist, just like the others, spoke excellent English and instantly put me at ease.

After the formalities of form filling and passport checking, he asked which room I would like from those available.

'Well, one with a great view would be delightful, especially as it's my first visit to Singapore. Would you choose for me?'

'I want you to have a lasting impression of our city,' he replied, and allocated me a room with a large panoramic window.

He passed me a message.

'Sunni will pick you up at ten tomorrow morning,'

I read.

Who the heck is Sunni? No way am I going off in a car with someone I've never even heard of! What if I end up as a sixty-year-old sex slave?

Seeing my consternation, the receptionist added that it was from someone called Siew Sai. Now the penny dropped! That was the name of David's business colleague, but as I had heard nothing from David, I'd forgotten all about him.

He remembered after all! Wonderful.

My head was churning with excitement as Ruby and I unpacked. I kicked Fred into a corner and wriggled my liberated toes.

'Oi, you! A little respect please,' he grumbled.

Now I understood that Siew Sai had asked Sunni, his driver and a local resident, to show me around Singapore. I was impatient for the adventure to begin, hoped Sunni spoke good English, and would include some of the places on my wish list.

Meanwhile I flicked through the hotel literature on the dressing table, wondering where to eat that evening. *Staying in for dinner would save me having to find a restaurant, but...*

I was still mulling it over when the desk clerk rang. *Might be a problem with my credit card...* flashed through my mind. Or worse, *Perhaps Sunni's not coming tomorrow after all?* Given my recent good fortune, it could be that I was being upgraded to a suite! I could always dream. No, he had a second message for me. I hadn't thought I was so popular.

'Mr. Siew Sai will be picking you up at seven this evening, madam. He is dining with business friends and hopes you will join them.'

It was getting better all the time! This busy man was troubling to take me to dinner with his associates. I wondered if they'd be discussing business that I wouldn't be party to. Maybe he considered I'd make the evening more entertaining, especially if they had never met an Irish woman before. Were they in for a shock or a treat? Take your pick. I wasn't sure.

I tried to imagine what Siew Sai would be like: a mature gentleman... a successful entrepreneur... he might be disappointed to find me a mature lady rather than a dynamic young business woman like the one in seat 1B? Ruby couldn't guess either, but then she didn't have much experience of such matters.

'Either way, just be on your best behaviour,' she said. 'You'd better not let David down!'

A dinner date! I mused. *This is exciting!* I tried to get a grip, stop fantasising and change out of my travel clothes. *Fast food or posh restaurant?* Likely to be the latter.

'Lucky there's a skirt and top and sandals shoved in my left-hand pocket, just in case,' Ruby reminded me. I hadn't worn them since the Esprit Club and the Peninsula Hotel, although I felt seriously underdressed both times.

I skipped my siesta, and tried to look as elegant as I could to make a good impression, which was not easy given my crushed and limited wardrobe. Then, I made the error of asking Ruby how I looked.

'Okay. I reckon you'll pass... for an oldie...' she chirped back.

What a cheek. I felt young as a spring chicken!

Seven o'clock found me in the lobby and full of trepidation, eyeing a distinguished man approach the reception desk. *Is he my 'date'?* The receptionist pointed in my direction and Siew Sai introduced himself. I was delighted.

'I hope you're happy to join my three overseas clients for dinner? Afterwards I'll show you a little of Singapore at night.'

David had reported that I was a lovely lady with a beautiful Irish accent. Was he talking about me? Now, I had to live up to that description.

He warned me that he had booked a famous but rather unusual restaurant. Sunni was waiting outside with the people carrier door open and the clients from Korea and Dubai settled happily inside. They welcomed me in fluent English, and I was relieved that Siew Sai would not have to spend his evening translating for my benefit, as well as playing host and tour guide.

I would never have come across this unique venue on my own. The Long Beach Marina Seafood Restaurant was enormous, packed full, and the decibels were through the roof. I had never seen so many diners gathered together in one restaurant; which reminded me of Piccadilly Circus on a Saturday night.

Each wall was lined with tanks containing various species of fish, and customers were busily checking out the information on each tank and inspecting the specimens before selecting the exact one to eat. The feeding of the five thousand flashed through my mind. I didn't have a clue what species most of them were, so it wasn't an entirely useful exercise, but it was interesting to watch the regulars who did know. It was fairly pricey though not pretentious, but if you fancy chicken, pork or beef don't go there because it is strictly pescatarian.

Siew Sai saw my baffled looks and came to the rescue by helping me choose. That was a relief and

I felt I had dodged a bullet, but when I enquired for cod, plaice, haddock or trout, he looked at me blankly as if I was speaking another language. And, in a way, I was. He was not familiar with any of my choices.

'Well, are you prepared to be adventurous?' he asked.

Up to a point, I thought, *but not eel, please!* Luckily, he did not propose eel. The establishment was famous for its signature dish, which was giant crab served in a chili and black pepper sauce. Not being a big fan of chilies, and being on the boring side, I played it safe and went for the king prawns. Once all our selections were laid out in front of us, I was speechless – most unusual for me. I had never seen such a display of assorted seafood, and marvelled at how we would eat it all.

My companions suggested that I sample each dish. It felt risky. On the other hand, I might never have this chance again, so I found the pluck. My eyes instantly watered at the black pepper and chilli sauce, which set off a brief bout of coughing soon abated by a glass of water, but which left my face chilli-red and silenced me for a while. Luckily, no one suggested I eat a whole crab or they'd have had a very quiet meal.

But I did have my first drink from a coconut and discovered that after you drink the liquid you eat the coconut flesh, making a refreshing drink and a dessert all in one. How novel is that? Whoever first pointed out that travelling is an education knew what they were talking about.

Not content with the all-in-one coconut, Siew Sai ordered a selection of five different desserts. Yes, five; he was definitely out to impress. Where were we supposed to put them? His idea was for us to taste each one. I was on a rampant sampling spree that night and particularly liked the mango mousse and black rice pudding with vanilla ice cream. I imagined Ruby on my shoulder warning me to keep the weight down so I could still trek with her.

The businessmen left us after dinner as they were leaving that night. I didn't envy them their flight after all that spicy food. Siew Sai suggested that he and I embark on a night tour of Singapore, taking in the Christmas lights on Orchard Road, and Little India. Despite my protestations about not taking up his time after such a lovely evening, he insisted. I could tell he was proud of being Singaporean and willingly gave in. I couldn't really have passed on an adventure like that.

Orchard Road is Singapore's equivalent to London's Regent Street. I was blown away by its magnificent Christmas decorations, which somewhat put our London lights into shadow. The roads were jam-packed, with no parking places, but as my host was driving, I had perfect views. He could only creep forward, which meant I could feast on the city's Christmas theme of illuminated musical instruments surrounded by crotchets, semi-quavers and treble clefs; the overhanging garlands were as original and beautiful as fairyland, and all sponsored by the Hitachi Company, which had been the case for many years. I was lost for words.

Of course, I had left my camera back at the hotel. How clever was that? I felt annoyed with myself and resolved to photograph the spectacle another night. We weren't finished yet, oh no! Siew Sai was a regular night owl and happy to keep partying, which is how we found ourselves exploring Little India.

On the way he filled me in about how this area came to be populated by Indian immigrants who fled to Singapore in the 1800s, to escape unrest in their homeland. There were constant wars and famines in India, so people stayed in Singapore where they set up shops and homes, leading to the development of a whole community. The brightly coloured shops and houses that reflect Indian culture so intoxicatingly give Little India a quite different ambience from the rest of the city.

The historic district was buzzing with vibrant culture and was a spirited shopping experience late into the night. People were eating or hanging out together as if it were mid-day, and my every sense lit up. Gold and silver bangles and other adornments sparkled from stalls around me. Henna artists were set up at the side of the road and ornamenting their punters' hands and feet with great concentration. Garlands of jasmine flowers, spices and cosmetics were changing hands, and my eye was caught by many a resplendent sari in swathes of vivid orange, vermillion, ruby red or gold. *Does anyone ever go to bed?* I marvelled.

The district also throngs with temples, open late into the evening, but I was not dressed suitably to go inside. I decided I would feel nervous going there on my own at night in case I got lost in the winding roads and alleys, and noticed far more men than women out on the streets. I imagined wandering down maze-like streets and disappearing into the darkness.

I do sometimes take risks when left to my own devices, because I like a bit of excitement. I can't help it. You may question my common sense. Am I foolhardy? Should I grow up and not get so carried away in my enthusiasm? The good news is that I'm still alive; it's not a ghost writing these pages. Self-confidence, you'll be pleased to hear, only takes me so far!

It had been an exhilarating day and I found myself asking how my guide was finding fresh energy at almost midnight, when we agreed it was time to drop me back at the hotel. All good things come to an end and I had been on the go for hours. Siew Sai had bestowed so much generosity on me, a complete stranger, and I needed to pinch myself when I listed all we had done since I walked out on Ruby and Fred. We said our goodnights and I thanked Siew Sai for a wonderful time.

'If you have no set plans for the morning, I'll ask Sunni to drive you to whichever sights you feel like visiting,' he said. And pre-empting me, he added, 'Please say yes. It would be our pleasure.'

When I quietly closed my bedroom door, I was cream-crackered (to use the Cockney) and hardly had energy to undress and fall into bed. I don't remember if I brushed my teeth. I do remember crying though, with a mixture of joy and sadness. I was very aware of how lucky I'd been to have such a warm introduction to Singapore by kind and generous acquaintances.

But I was awoken from my deep sleep. After my long and exciting evening, it took a while to wake up and orientate myself *What's that noise? Why is the sky so bright?*

I soon identified the deafening sound of thunder, and lightning. The clock at my bedside showed that it was three in the morning. I have always been a scaredy-cat when it comes to storms, but this time I was so exhausted that I fell straight back to sleep in moments.

Chapter 13

THE IRISHMAN'S SULTAN MOSQUE

Next moment the phone was ringing and the receptionist reminded me that Siew Sai's driver would arrive at ten.

I had no time for breakfast and was out of my nightdress in a flash and soon in a pair of jeans, a top and Fred. I splashed my face and cleaned my teeth. *That's it – I'm ready!* No time to doll myself up, not that it would make much difference. My mother used to see me trying to be glamorous to go dancing, and her ego-building remarks knew no bounds!

'Brigid, you can't make a silk purse out of a sow's ear.'

I helped myself from the fruit bowl and packed some bottled water before flying out of the room like a banshee and rushing down for another adventurous day. I must have looked a bit rough.

Greeting me by the front desk was the cheerful smiling Sunni, and alongside him stood an elegantly suited and sun-hatted woman. With a beaming smile Melinda introduced herself as Siew Sai's personal assistant, and explained that she would be my guide for the day. Siew Sai had allocated her a day to show me around. A lovely thought.

Melinda enquired if I had any special requests, but I left it completely up to her, instinctively knowing that whatever she showed me would be memorable. Right from the start we got on like a house on fire: Sunni was a jolly and attentive driver, Melinda was the consummate guide, and she treated me like a princess.

'Have you met the Queen?' she asked with innocent interest.

I explained that you had to be a very important or special person to meet the Queen, but that I had visited Buckingham Palace and watched the Coldstream Guards, in their furry bearskin headwear, performing the Changing of the Guard ceremony.

She told me that she longed to visit famous places she had heard about, like the Tower of London and Westminster Abbey, and see a play at a West End theatre. And, naturally, I offered to show her around if she made it over.

Our first destination was the Arab quarter where I was excited to notice an authentic Middle Eastern vibe, the air saturated with a smell of aromatic spices. It's a strange world and, bizarrely, I learned that the Sultan Mosque here was designed by Denis Santry, an Irishman. I had come all the way to Singapore to find an impressive Arab mosque, built in the Indo-Saracenic style by an architect and engineer who hailed from Cork. It personalised the outing in a new way.

Our next stop was the waterfront where Melinda showed me a splendid statue of Sir Stamford Raffles, the founder of Singapore as a city port in 1819, who worked as a British colonial agent for the East India Company. A memorial statue of him still stands in Westminster Abbey too.

During the hours I spent with Melinda I asked endless questions about the city-port's history. I was fascinated, and Sunni waited patiently, unremittingly upbeat and chatty, until we were pleasantly interrupted by a call from Siew Sai who suggested we meet him for lunch at a Chinese restaurant nearby.

When Siew Sai greeted us, he explained that we would be eating with Nish, his office partner, and Amitava, a business friend from Delhi. He was obviously skillful at combining business with pleasure and had it off to a fine art. The men were polite but reserved, and I imagined them wondering who was this whacky Irish woman Siew Sai had befriended? However, I tried even more new dishes and had an excellent meal. I was growing braver and more adventurous by the hour.

To top it off, Siew Sai had booked me into his health club for a back massage and reflexology. I was so excited and couldn't wait for some blissful pampering before wafting off to sleep under the soothing hands of a masseuse... or even, perhaps, a masseur?

I should have known better by now. Not having experienced reflexology, I did not anticipate the pain I was about to be put through, but soon remembered the voice of my friend Pat who warned me gently that certain massages could be 'quite an experience'. I was about to find out why she had not gone into detail, although I probably would not have believed her anyway and had been in no mood to read between the lines. Once again, I was lulled into complacency by the smiling faces and jovial natures of young men who were planning to put me through hell. Once they had done their worst, they reported that I'd had a lot of toxins to get rid of and that my diet was poor. Melinda and I drove back to Siew Sai's office, where he invited me to join his family that evening for his son's tenth birthday at their country club.

At last, I met his wife, Meili, a petite woman with shiny long black hair, who welcomed us at the club with Joel, Ethan and Joshua, their boys. The eight-, ten- and twelve-year-old's were smartly turned out for the birthday treat and self-assured, even somewhat reserved by British standards, but they were well-mannered with excellent social skills. They were unphased by the intruder at the family dinner. Perhaps I was a novelty, being from England, although the family was clearly comfortable with overseas visitors. We chatted a little about golf and they told me that they played in the junior section.

Siew Sai whispered that he had ordered a surprise for his chocolate-loving middle boy. Ethan's eyes lit up when the chef presented him with a long crocodile-shaped chocolate cake and he was grinning from ear to ear after he blew out the candles and his mother cut generous slices for all of us. He was like the cat who got the cream! It was a memorable picture for the family album.

I felt honoured to be part of it, particularly as I

had only met Siew Sai two days previously. They introduced me to other club members and I was treated like royalty. Having already raised the subject of golf, the topic of my golfing handicap came up with every person I met. It wasn't a case of, 'This is Brigid, an Irish friend who's travelling round the world', but 'This is Brigid and she plays off a handicap of ten'. It was another first for me, being pitched preeminently as a golfer. Meili's warm and hospitable nature made me feel so included, and I wondered if all Singaporean women were this kind. And no – she did not play golf.

The boys had put up with enough adult conversation for one evening so Meili took them home as it was getting late. But Siew Sai and I went off to collect Amitava, and we ended up at the famous Raffles Hotel for cocktails. That man packs so much into a day and never seems tired!

Mr Ngiam Tong Boon, bartender, made the Raffles Long Bar renowned worldwide when he created his 'Singapore Sling' back in 1915. It is a perfectly-balanced mix of gin, Cointreau, pineapple juice and fresh lime juice. Well, we had to try one, didn't we?

The atmosphere was vibrant, with a live band and conspicuously fashionable customers. It was like a fairytale and I really enjoyed being part of it for a while, though I couldn't help noticing an explosion of peanut shells all over the floor and tables; everywhere I looked. This is apparently the norm at the Raffles; a sort of decadence you read about but never see. I forget how many cocktails we downed, but I know we left around midnight, passing back through the musical Christmas lights so I could take pictures.

It was one in the morning when I arrived back to Ruby.

'So, where exactly have *you* been?' asked Ruby.

'Out on the town... and whyever not?' I answered. She rustled her canvas and settled down again.

When I came down to breakfast a gorgeous hunk of a young man led me to the table, pulled out a chair and, with a stunning smile, placed a napkin on my lap. It flashed through my mind to ask if he was married, but I flashed it out of my mind very fast! Instead, I asked what he would recommend for breakfast. 'Leave it with me, madam,' he said, and returned with a pleasing selection of fresh fruit, yoghurt, pastries and fresh coffee, followed up by a mushroom omelette. This was already turning into a good day. He really cheered me up.

As we had struck up a friendly rapport I was almost tempted to ask if he was free for the evening.

'Dream on...' murmured Fred, begrudgingly, from under the table.

I let that particular fantasy slip away and moved onto more respectable ground by asking if he knew where the Catholic Cathedral was. Yes, he did; it was the oldest in Singapore, and he told me how to get there. I had resolved to attend Mass every Sunday, and I would. That's the Irish Catholic in me – well trained.

'And what about the Singapore Botanical Gardens?'

'Absolutely,' he said. 'It's a beautiful place... and the orchids are mind-blowing!'

Well, that was me sorted for the day! I left the table a happy bunny, and practically hopped out of the dining room.

Singapore's Cathedral of the Good Shepherd was first established in 1832 by French missionaries, but rebuilt in its present splendour with architecture influenced by both Saint Paul's, Covent Garden and Saint Martin-in-the-Fields, in London. During WWII it was used as an emergency hospital. By pure luck I found a pew near the front and had a direct view of the choir, whose harmonies sent shivers down my spine, accompanied by the oldest pipe organ in the country.

I noticed wall plaques commemorating the early

European missionaries and learned that the Good Shepherd still has an active Korean congregation, harking back to an era of Korean Catholic martyrs in Singapore. The atmosphere and enthusiasm of the choir was electrifying and their well-rehearsed contribution to the Mass was its highlight, one that created an oasis of calm.

Wanting to maintain my peaceful state of mind, I felt drawn to the botanical gardens, now a UNESCO World Heritage Site. I couldn't have chosen better. I love walking anyway, so a couple of hours wandering around these tropical gardens was right up my street! It is so much more than a garden: a delightful blend of walking trails, lakes, waterfalls, special collections, and majestic trees that are hundreds of years old – and each one is labelled.

Just as my handsome waiter had said, its supreme attraction is the Rolls Royce of orchid collections, for which experience alone the entrance fee is well worth it. The vibrancy and richness of the orchids' colours took my breath away!

I have a friend whose husband, Ed, collects and tends orchids on wide kitchen window sills packed with different varieties; so many shapes and species in a blaze of colour. I called to mind the two orchids I received as a birthday present from a well-meaning friend who could not believe that I only have to look at a plant to kill it. Those victim plants knew their days were numbered under my lack of tender care and gave up the ghost. You can imagine how neglected they would have been if Ed had not charged to rescue them just as they were teetering on their last legs. Ed, the orchid doctor, carried them away to his botanical intensive care unit and revived them. It became routine: whenever I went on holiday my orchids went on holiday too – not with me – they went to Ed's for pampering and TLC.

The meticulous design of the Singapore Botanical Gardens was originally drawn up by a series of Kew-trained specialists. If you ever happen to be in Singapore, put it on your list; the 82 hectares, varying between bonsai gardens and an international ginger collection to Swan and Symphony Lakes, Palm Valley and a Walk of Giants, will transport you from the hustle and bustle outside. And even if you think you know orchids, you will never have seen orchids like these.

The concierge had arranged transport for my Quantas flight to Brisbane at nine that evening and once on the shuttle I rehearsed the lasting memories of my fabulous stay. Everything had been spotless and orderly, ran on time, easily accessible, with no pushing or shoving to raise any uneasiness. Everyone I was introduced to through David had lifted my Singapore days from the special to the extraordinary.

I teased myself with dreams of another upgrade, but knew it was wishful thinking. Either way, I was on my way to Australia now and I was on a roll.

Chapter 14

FOR MEN ONLY

I headed for the Quantas Desk to check in for Brisbane and was handed my ticket by the surliest person I'd come across for days. It was quite a shock. *Shall I recommend a course in social skills on my feedback form?* No upgrade hinted at here then.

This straight-faced efficiency trend continued all the way to Brisbane. Business Class was populated by men apart from me. From the word go I experienced no culture of offering or customer care, and had to request whatever I needed. *Ruby*, I thought, *if you're listening from your locker, you'll be horrified at how I'm being ignored!*

But as for the man beside me, well, the flight attendant was fawning all over him. Had she been denied her vocation as an escort? Or even a hooker? (I was seriously out of sorts by now and couldn't make up my mind which suited her better.) He was clearly flattered, flirting like mad, and maybe even wondering if he might get his leg over tonight. Did I really think that? Well, yes! Sexual inference was oozing from her in bucket-loads and I wouldn't have been surprised at an impending initiation to the Mile-High Club for him. *Gullible sod!* I heard myself thinking. I think you get the gist. I was not a happy bunny.

It was a drawn-out journey of comparative neglect with mediocre refreshments, and I was glad to disembark. I thought this disappointing experience of Quantas was over. But I was wrong: the next leg, from Brisbane to Cairns, was on this very plane, the only saving grace being a change of flight crew. Months later I did write to the Quantas CEO about refresher courses for his cabin staff. Guess what? I haven't yet received an acknowledgement, much less the apology he is probably composing. So, dear reader, I rest my case with you.

The views flying between Brisbane and Cairns resettled my mind. The Great Barrier Reef was an exhilarating sight on which my eyes and camera remained glued. I now appreciated why it is one of the Seven Wonders of the World, more extensive than the Great Wall of China! *Something to tell the grandchildren*, I thought, *...but they probably know already.*

As we touched down, I grew uncontrollably excited about meeting Brenda, my birthday twin, who would be waiting for me. It only seemed yesterday that she sparked the idea of joining her celebrations, and so much had arisen from that chance meeting at the Surrey golf club.

And there she was, running towards me, her arms wide open and grinning from ear to ear! She gave me such a welcome hug that I was overwhelmed. Somehow, I had never quite imagined that our long-planned meeting would become reality. Her partner, Peter, stood on the sidelines as we greeted each other. I was overcome with ambivalence; a deep sadness that Michael wasn't there, and joy that I was. I will never forget that moment until the day I die!

Over the hour's drive to Port Douglas, I came down to earth and met Peter properly. Passing close to the ocean provided a fresh perspective on the reef's shimmering turquoise waters, with mountains on the other side of the road forming a backdrop.

At last, this day had come! After so many escapades I was finally here in Queensland. Brenda took me on an introductory tour to the pretty marina and long sandy beach. *No one's swimming...* I noticed, before plucking up the courage to ask why.

'Oh no. Never! You'd be taking your life in your hands to swim here,' Brenda explained. 'It's full of salt water crocodiles... the dangerous kind. They visit us at Four Mile Beach sometimes.'

I certainly would not be dipping so much as a toe into that tempting blue sea!

The small town of Port Douglas gives easy access to both the Great Barrier Reef and the Daintree Rainforest, a national park. The vegetation is lush and tropical giving a knock-on effect of pretty high humidity levels. It took some getting used to with frequent cold showers and longing to jump under the water again before even drying off.

It's a pretty place, set on the Coral Sea and renowned for fantastic restaurants that I was keen to try out. Brenda had designated her kitchen as out of bounds for the week. Wait a minute – that's not strictly true. When a G and T or a glass of chilled wine was needed... well, naturally she made an exception! Luckily, Peter was very obliging at whipping up a neat meal when hunger struck.

Meanwhile, Brenda and I passed the time chatting like excited teenagers, telling each other how surreal it all felt, and praising the determination of my daughters who persuaded me to take a chance.

'I'm warning you, we're going to have one hell of a celebration,' said Brenda. 'I've made so many plans that it's going to last all week!'

As she recited her plans, an almighty clap of thunder sounded overhead, followed by a bolt of lightning. The heavens opened and much-needed rain cascaded down – it was the first they had seen in two months. Had I brought it with me as a gift? With the onset of wetter conditions, Brenda advised spraying myself with Bushman's' or Aeroguard insect repellent as soon as I finished showering in the mornings if I didn't want give the mozzies a feast; it was the first I'd heard of these heavy-duty repellents that target tropical pests.

'With all this rain there's nothing for it but a glass of bubbly before dinner. How about it?' she asked.

'I thought perhaps you'd gone tee-total,' I teased, '...but you can twist my arm.' And she did.

So, after sipping our champagne, we headed off to On the Inlet, a restaurant with a long-standing reputation for its seafood. It felt comfortable as soon as we walked in. With welcoming smiles, the waiter showed us to a table that had eye-dazzling views of the Dickson Inlet.

I asked the same waiter for a recommendation and he suggested the Spanish mackerel. Now, I am not a great fan of mackerel but seeing my crestfallen face he reassured me.

'No worries, it's nothing like UK mackerel. Ours has soft white flesh... it's far and away the tastiest of the mackerel family.'

And, of course, he was right; it was delicious, and perfected by washing it down with a New Zealand Sauvignon Blanc.

Back home Peter made fresh coffee with liqueur nightcaps, and by eleven o'clock we were ready to stock up on sleep before the big bash – in just over forty-eight hours – on our joint sixtieth birthdays.

As I lay in my bed that night it brought memories of when alcohol had played an overpowering part in my life with Michael; when we went to AA and Al-Anon meetings and learned to live "one day at a time".

But alcohol is, nonetheless, part of everyday life, even though the disease of alcoholism can creep up unknowingly on anyone. At restaurants, parties, celebrations and family gatherings, or when simply catching up with friends, alcohol is normally available.

Like most people, I enjoy a drink. But having been married to an alcoholic I realise how addictive it can become if you allow it to. It is no respecter of colour, age, class, wealth or education. It can destroy friendships, relationships, careers, and families.

Al-Anon meetings taught me how to be happy and make my own choices, whether or not Michael was drinking. I chose to abstain even when he couldn't, and I continued that abstinence for a while once he was sober, out of sensitivity to his effort. After some time, he let me know that it did not cause him problems being with me or friends who were enjoying a drink. He acknowledged his own accountability and accepted his own power.

'If I decide on a drink, no one will stop me. It has to be my decision,' he confided.

Once Michael gained sobriety, he never drank alcohol again and spent the remainder of his life helping others through their own dark times. We continued to attend Al-Anon and AA meetings and some of the people we bonded with became lifelong friends. We now enjoyed a close family life together and, as time went by, I drank socially with friends. But I knew what alcohol addiction could do, and I knew how to say "no thank you".

Chapter 15

DANCING WITH ANDREW

I woke up on top of the world having slept like a baby. My flight experience with Quantas was history.

'From here on in, it's party time,' I told Ruby. 'I might even pop you through the wash for the occasion... and give Fred a brush-up too.'

'We're out here... in the sun room. Come and join us!' rang Brenda's voice. As I joined her at the back of the house for my first coffee, Peter arrived carrying a scented wooden crate.

'Look what's been delivered... your name on it, Brenda.'

It was his first of several presents, and a tropical fruity aroma wafted our way when he lifted the lid. It was a box of mangoes! I had never seen a mango before. (I know, I've led a sheltered life.) The smell was heady like an exotic perfume and has been unmistakable ever since.

'You've not lived if you haven't tasted a mango!' said Brenda.

I watched as Peter expertly peeled one for my delight. Yes, like everything else, there is a knack for peeling a mango, or you get in a right mess and end up dripping in sticky yellow juice. It was silky smooth. And the smell? Heavenly. After I'd finished swooning over my mango he brought in a scrumptious selection of pastries and preserves.

So, the three of us were in excellent form to head into town where I revelled in the bohemian character that teemed with arts and craft shops, street stalls, independent fashion boutiques, cafés and eating stops. We sauntered along Four Mile Beach by a turquoise sea without a care in the world, and when the trawlers came in we bought king prawns, scallops and a selection of fresh fish to grill later on the barbecue.

Back home we took a casual dip in the pool, and emerged to another glass of chilled wine before getting dressed to meet Brenda's other guests, who were arriving in advance of the next day's partying. My thoughts drifted all over the place. *Could I get used to this way of life and tell the family I'm emigrating to Australia?*

That evening the conversation flowed effortlessly, nurtured by Peter's top-class barbecue skills. I was happily surprised to reconnect with old golfing friends from Chipstead as well as meeting Peter's mate, Andrew, who was over from London. I forget when we went to sleep, but I do remember how much we enjoyed the food, wine and banter.

'I met Andrew, he's really dishy,' I told Ruby, as she hung damply upside down in the shower, nearly dry and smelling much better.

'I hope he's not replacing me? Am I going to end up redundant?'

'Not likely! You won't end up on the baggage heap,' I reassured her, as I removed the pegs and smoothed her canvas. 'You come first.'

And then we were waking up on Brenda's Big Day. Happy Birthday Brenda! Although my birthday was before I started out on my voyage, we had agreed to mark the day together and had both resolved to be sixty years' young. I would have missed so many life-changing adventures if Brenda had not extended her invitation and propelled me to the other side of the world.

We girls were booked to start the day at Breakfast with the Birds, a venue in the Habitat Nature Reserve.

I couldn't help wondering which would be noisiest, and even suggested placing bets.

We sat in a wetlands' environment, surrounded by the babble and jangle of its aerial residents who showed off their kaleidoscopic plumage from their perches as we breakfasted on tropical fruits, freshly-baked breads and pastries, and a selection of hot food, as well as fresh juices, teas and coffee. The gaudy and brazen parrots fed off our tables, and one even dipped its beak into my apple juice. Luckily, I don't suffer from ornithophobia!

Once fed and watered, we were taken into the nature reserve where I cuddled a koala bear! It was the cutest of creatures but quite heavy to hold, and had seriously sharp toenails. I was glad the keeper stayed at hand. I also saw my first cassowary, which looks not unlike a turkey. Cassowaries, I discovered, are native flightless birds with blue and red heads, and a skin-covered casque on the crown that grows as they age. We saw cockatoos, lorikeets, crocodiles, wallabies and kangaroos, all looking happy in their own custom-made environments. Having breakfast with nature was the best possible start to the day.

Our young guide showed a deep interest. She was well-informed and you could tell how much she enjoyed her job. I felt she might even have done it voluntarily from her obvious love of the creatures in her care. I have never spent a birthday in such an exotic location, and it took my breath away. I'm unlikely to ever again experience a birthday present like it. The morning passed in the blink of an eye. Time flies like that sometimes, doesn't it?

While we were enjoying ourselves, the men were at home setting up trestle tables and a sound system around the barbecue area and pool in readiness for the festivities. They had done a great job, oiled with a few beers to help them on.

'If you can't beat them... well, join them,' we agreed, as one woman. So, being five o'clock somewhere, it seemed appropriate to crack open the champagne! Having personally selected the stunning array of fish, and being the only one who knew how to cook it, Peter was in charge of the barbecue.

We ate a glut of oysters, king prawns, mud crabs, and Morton Bay Bugs (which are not the pests they sound like but tasted like small lobsters). All were a delicious discovery for me.

'Peter, your restaurant has earned five stars tonight!' I told him. 'Brenda should definitely hang on to you!'

Early in the evening more friends arrived, ones who had been working or had turned up ad hoc.

Some came ready dressed in swimwear so they could cool off in and out of the plunge pool. I met Tom and Patricia, who live in Port Douglas but also have an apartment in Sydney.

I told them that I was heading for Sydney, and they suggested we could maybe meet for lunch at Doyle's restaurant. I remember Siobhan telling me I should try to eat at Doyle's in Watson's Bay (she likes a good five-star restaurant), although I may not be lucky enough to get a booking. That old adage of privilege was true: its not what you know, its who you know. It seemed that Tom and Patricia had a table whenever they wanted one.

We swapped phone numbers – it felt like an offer I could not possibly turn down.

Music was in full swing by now, and we were each dancing in our own version of the art. Dishy Andrew was one of the latecomers. He was a fantastic dancer and he and I had a ball together! I felt fluttering wings as if I were a teenager. I must have been nuts, but the alcohol certainly loosened up my inhibitions! He was a good fifteen years younger than me but, not only did we dance brilliantly together, there was a strong sense of being at ease in each other's company. Even though we started as strangers, it ended as if we had known each other for ever.

Nothing made sense, but why question it on such a euphoric occasion? In younger days I was always dancing, especially jiving, and was often the last to leave the floor.

The party finally wound down around nine o'clock, but we were ready for more.

'Who's coming to finish off the day at the yacht club?' asked Peter.

My new dancing partner was game for it. We had clicked and, ironically, his sense of humour was very similar to Michael's. We were having such a great time and were pretty well oblivious to anyone else. You could have lit up a palace with the electricity between us.

At the yacht club we swapped snippets about our lives. Andrew was divorced, and visiting Port Douglas specifically to see Peter and celebrate Brenda's birthday. He was leaving next morning for Sydney to meet his daughter who was over from England. Even back at the house we drank coffee and chatted until we went to bed in the early hours. No, not together! That would have been totally out of order. After all, we were both guests in someone else's home, which was most likely a good thing.

Importantly, Brenda and I enjoyed our party no end and will treasure fond shared memories. Thank you, Andrew, for adding so much to the fun and excitement. I will certainly remember!

Why did I have to meet him this early on in my widowhood? I immediately knew I could not live with the guilt of feeling disloyal to my husband, who would always be at the forefront of my mind and affections. Our meeting was a case of the wrong place and wrong time. As much as we were attracted to each other, I was not ready or comfortable about taking it to another level. *C'est la vie*.

Chapter 16

WAVING OR DROWNING?

Brenda is bubbly by nature and does not need an excuse to let her hair down, which meant our festivities were by no means finished – oh no! She had another surprise in store.

I was sipping coffee in the sun room, when she announced a treehouse lunch for fourteen at Silky Oaks Lodge. They were sending a limo to ferry us both ways, so we didn't need a designated driver. Marvellous! A free pass to take the hair of the dog!

The Treehouse Restaurant is set on stilts high in the rainforest canopy. Sporting a roof, but no glass windows or screens, it provides the magical sensation of eating outside in the middle of the jungle. Like Brenda herself, the venue was stylish and elegant. As well as enveloping us in lush foliage it gave breathtaking sights of the Mossman River flowing deep below.

'Time to put on your swimming costume!' announced Brenda, when we got home.

'Be scared, Brigid! You know you can't swim,' warned Ruby.

I visualised a spot of sunbathing, with an occasional dip in the pool to cool down, then lazing on a sun lounger as we chatted about seeing the Great Barrier Reef next morning. But that was not what Brenda had planned for me at all. As I walked out, dressed for relaxation and with Ruby carrying my small towel and sunscreen, Brenda thrust some unfamiliar apparatus into my hands.

'Come on! I'm teaching you how to snorkel. You'll need to do it tomorrow at the Barrier Reef.'

Why the hell would I want to snorkel in the Great Barrier Reef? I thought. *Can't I just peer over the side of the boat?*

'What are you thinking?' squealed Ruby. 'I'll be an orphan, and how will I get back home when you've drowned?'

'Oh no, Brenda. I'm sorry, but I'm not a strong swimmer,' I pleaded. 'I hate putting my head under the water...'

'Brigid, just follow my instructions and do exactly as I say.' She wasn't having any of it. 'Everything will go... well, just swimmingly.'

I had no choice other than to trust her and pray for the best. *Please don't let me drown,* I begged silently. *I've got too much going for me!*

'Ruby...' I forced out the words, 'I am absolutely certain that Brenda won't let me sink.' But I didn't really have that much faith.

After spending what felt like six months in the pool, and listening to Brenda's every tiny instruction, I was shattered. I think she was surprised and relieved that I eventually unwound enough to master the art of breathing properly; I know I was. Yippee! She said I had done well for a novice and would cope fine out at sea tomorrow. I admired her patience and perseverance but I wished I had her confidence. I could hear Siobhan trying to impress some reality on me, 'Don't be stupid. It took me over a year to qualify for snorkelling and sea diving in the sea... not three hours in a swimming pool!'

I couldn't sleep for worrying how on earth, after three hours practicing in a garden pool, I could submerge my head in the ocean surrounded by millions of fish.

'Sharks too,' Ruby remembered.

'What the hell am I going to do?'

'I don't bloody know! It was your idea to do the Great Barrier Reef thing, not mine.'

'I don't think I'll feel well enough in the morning. I can't snorkel if I'm not up to scratch...' I was madly plotting to save my blushes and dignity.

'How can you get out of it now?' Ruby said. She had a point. 'And I'll have aided and abetted the drowning by carrying your stuff!'

'Rise and shine!' called Brenda, up the stairs.

I couldn't face breakfast because my insides were churning in trepidation. But, like it or not, I was to take the plunge. Friday 2nd December is washed with colours in my brain: the Great Barrier Reef in its wondrous and terrifying glory!

Brenda warned me it would be a packed day, as we drove to the harbour. She had booked a small boat out to the reef so I would receive individual attention. The company was geared up for people like me who were new to diving. To be on the safe side, she and her friend would act as my dive buddies; my 'minders', to stop me being eaten by sharks.

'I don't fancy explaining to your children: 'Sorry, I lost your mother somewhere on the Great Barrier Reef!'' she said.

And I did feel in safe hands. We waited at the harbour entrance, entranced by all sizes and shapes of boats coming and going, while Brenda checked in.

She had advised me to wear a long-sleeved T-shirt, shorts over my swimming costume, and not to forget a sun hat and change of clothes. Sunscreen was strictly forbidden because the chemicals in it destroy marine life.

As we boarded, in Port Douglas, I felt my heart beating with alternate thumps: one in anxiety and the next in exhilaration. I was relieved to find very few punters on board. I hoped I'd be less nervous. *Just get out to sea*, I was praying. *I can't chicken out then.*

Reaching the reef waters took an hour and a half, but we were entertained by pods of dolphins and their babies swimming in front of our boat. It was the nearest I'd been to a dolphin and I was enchanted at how gracefully they danced in the water.

We helped ourselves to a selection of soft drinks and cakes (a buffet was coming at lunchtime) as we sailed on to a secluded part of the first of three reefs. Before our first jump into the waters, a crew member who was a marine biologist told us about the fish species we could expect to spot.

We divided into snorkellers and two scuba divers. In my imagination I toyed with being one of the scuba divers; magically being promoted from complete newbie to an expert diver, but in my head,

I still heard Siobhan saying, 'Mum, please get real... you can't even swim properly!'

So, instead, my designated minders and the crew helped me down the steps and into the water. I could see the crew were used to beginners and understood my fear, and were it not for their wonderful empathy I would not have found the courage to get wet, minders or not! They insisted I wear a life belt, not wanting to return to shore an Irishwoman short. Once in the softly lapping ocean I felt myself relaxing, being mesmerised by the display of sea life and always flanked by Brenda and Angie, just in case I went AWOL.

Angelfish, with their distinctive winged shape and striking colourful stripes, were the awe-inspiring species I remember most vividly. And Butterfly Fish too; bright yellow relatives of the Angels, with their eye-like black spots. When the bright orange and white Clownfish swam past, I couldn't help but think of Marlin in *Finding Nemo*. The shoals of Damselfish were a mass of stunning electric blue, but easily startled back into crevices in the reef, whereas, by contrast, the wide-mouthed grouper, Queensland's largest bony fish, swim slowly, ponderously and unphased by we divers. Their magic was such that I was wholly absorbed, transported in a sea of wonder where I forgot that I was snorkelling. If you get the chance to look at these amazing ocean dwellers on Google, you'll feel something of their glorious shapes and colours without even getting splashed!

Back on the boat I pinched myself. *Have I really bathed in the breathtaking beauty of the world's largest coral reef... visible from outer space?* When we sailed back into Port Douglas I was still bursting with elation and regaled anyone who would listen with my valiant feat. Friends beckoned us for a drink at the yacht club, but we declined. We just wanted a relaxing supper with Peter and to tell him every detail of our day.

That underwater kaleidoscope will be with me as long as I live. Immersing my face to share the waters of the Great Barrier Reef with its natural population would have been unimaginable a week earlier, and yet there I was happily snorkelling for an hour at each of three different sites. I sensed my wild Irish streak reappearing. I was learning never to say 'never' because fresh abilities surface as we age. I watch the *Blue Planet* in a totally different light these days, as one of millions who actively strive towards raising awareness of how we are destroying biomes like the Great Barrier Reef by putting ourselves above nature. I could also hear myself making a special boast to my children and grandchildren: *Watch this space and be proud. Your grandmother is only on the starting blocks!*

Chapter 17

SKY WALKING

How to follow yesterday? It can't get any better, so prepare for it to go downhill! I lay in bed trying to recapture the previous day, wondering if it really happened. I had spent the night swimming in a warm ocean of charmed dreams and was not ready to engage with breakfast until nine. I felt blessed to have shared yesterday with such a caring friend.

As my adrenaline settled over coffee, Peter revealed he too had a trick up his sleeve. He told me about the world's oldest surviving tropical rainforest, which is only forty-three miles north of Port Douglas and covers 460 square miles. The Daintree Forest is a UNESCO World Heritage Site comprising Daintree National Park, the Daintree River and Mossman Gorge that we had glimpsed from the Treehouse restaurant. The protected ecosystem is home to plants and animals found nowhere else on earth.

'So, down your coffee, grab another pastry, and let's be off!' he announced.

A comfortable car seat was the perfect way to appreciate the incomparable scenery we drove into. Daintree is formed of rugged mountain peaks and gorges, quiet rivers and noisily crashing waterfalls, like the Roaring Meg Falls, and it stretches to the coast where canopied boardwalks link tropical rainforest with white sandy beaches fringed by reefs. At least 430 species of birds are known to thrive in the forest, including the endangered Southern Cassowaries that I'd recently met. It is named after the Victorian, Cambridge-educated geologist and photographer, Richard Daintree, and offers protection to 30% of the frogs, reptiles and kangaroos in Australia, as well as 90% of the bats and butterflies.

Once out of the car, things only got better and better. From a total of nineteen primitive flowering plant families recorded on earth, twelve are in the Daintree region. Canopy walking trails start in the heavily foliaged forest floor and climb over bridges at different levels, gradually meeting the light as it spills through the tree tops. We were surrounded by the sounds of birds, insects and animals, even when they were hidden from view. I had never walked in a rainforest, so my mind was blown by these canopied boardwalks that allowed us to glimpse wildlife, turquoise sea, and mile upon mile of sandy beaches.

After we had drunk in all we could absorb from the rainforest, Peter drove us to Mossman Gorge where the water is crystal clear and fed by an underground spring. It's a sheltered swimming hole, where the Mossman River flows over massive granite boulders, is surrounded by rainforest and enticingly secluded. We paddled in the refreshing clear water, using its boulders as stepping stones and being careful not to slip.

It was filled with many-coloured birds and so restful that I would have happily stayed for hours, but back at Port Douglas we were going out for a night on the town to celebrate another birthday; Brenda's friend Jan. Her husband was treating us to dinner at Nautilus, *the* restaurant in Port Douglas.

No one wanted the evening to end, but our car arrived and took us in style back to Brenda's for coffee and nightcap.

Andrew stayed overnight. We'd had a fantastic time and were both sorry he was leaving.

'Tonight, was a real bonus... sharing your company again,' he told me privately. 'Do you think we could meet again... maybe back in the UK?'

After breakfast he caught his flight to Sydney.

I tried to isolate a single outstanding memory. It was a tough choice between the birthday celebrations, the reef, rainforest, or maybe it was to be Andrew. I never did choose, but one sentiment was outstandingly clear: eternal gratitude for whoever stole my golf clubs all those years ago, because they indisputably enhanced my life! But then, I reminded myself, this wasn't the first time my life had indisputably changed.

Chapter 18

A CHILD IN KILKENNY

I was born in Kilkenny but grew up in the countryside, in Johnswell, where I attended the local convent before leaving for boarding school.

We were educated by nuns, some of whom were extraordinarily vicious and cruel. It was customary in Ireland of those times that one male child would become a priest and one female would become a nun. I think some of them must have resented their fate when they were only young girls with normal dreams. Maybe it felt like a punishment, and so they deflected their resentment onto those of us whose lives were less restricted.

In Johnswell, I became adept at climbing trees for conkers and cob nuts, picking wild strawberries, fighting the wasps for plums in the local farmer's orchard, swimming in rivers, learning to ride on a man's bike, and scrounging rides on hay carts. They were mostly carefree times. I spent school holidays outside - playing all day and only coming home when it started to get dark. I was always a country child at heart.

During the holidays, from the age of six or so, my evening chore was to walk a couple of miles with a billycan to collect milk from the Purcells' large dairy farm. Old Mr. Purcell had a soft spot for me. He had four sons but never a daughter, so was especially kind and always gave me sweets to munch on my way home.

One particular walk home with the milk is permanently etched in my memory. I was passing a field where a herd of cows and a bull were grazing. The bull charged at the fence for me, and I was so terrified that the billycan fell from my hand, spilling over my shoes and flowing down the road in a stream of waste. My first thoughts were how to explain this to my mother? I fretted about it all the way home. She didn't give me a chance to explain how scared I'd been, but simply took the belt off its hook on the wall and hit me with it. Mother was the disciplinarian in our family, and normally used the leather belt to discipline my brothers when she considered they had misbehaved. I never forgot what she did that night, irrespective of my tender age, and have not understood or forgiven her yet. After the beating, she sent me all the way back to the farm to refill the can.

Mr. Purcell was shocked when he saw me.

'Have you lost your best friend, Brigid?' he asked in consternation.

I told him my tale of woe and, taking pity on me, he summoned one of his boys.

'You see this young lady back home... and don't be spilling a drop from that can.'

It was the custom in those days to name the oldest grandson after his grandfather, which is why I remember that the lad, Tom Purcell, being named after his grandfather, and the oldest daughter after her grandmother. Being my mother's first girl, I was a Brigid.

Except for school holidays I spent Monday to Friday living with Brigid, my paternal grandmother, in Kilkenny, because I could walk to school from her house.

Looking back at that, I can honestly say I left my home and family at the age of six, which left me with no real connection with my two sisters. We had little in common apart from the same parents, but that was where the rapport ended. I missed my father mostly, because he was such a gentle kind man.

My grandmother was a retired headmistress, and the best math's teacher I ever had. She gave me my love of numbers as she had such memorable ways of explaining. Every evening she would give me a math's problem to solve. Most times, it was beyond me. But instead of berating me, humiliating me, or making me feel stupid, she painstakingly explained the sequence of steps I needed to arrive at a successful outcome.

During those early years, one of the nuns, in her wisdom, decided that I had academic potential. She gave me extra tuition and entered me for a county scholarship. I imagine the motivation was about the kudos of the school rather than sheer altruism, but a scholarship could bring about free education for the rest of my school life.

So, I studied hard and won one of the five County Kilkenny scholarships that allowed my parents a choice of schools and I hoped to make father proud of me. I was eight years old by then and very excited to be considered good enough for boarding school. Unfortunately, it didn't go as I hoped and turned into a horrible experience, especially hard to handle given my age.

The sticking point was that my mother chose a

convent where her sister was Mother Superior. It was away in Dublin, almost eighty miles from home, but where my education would not set them back a penny until I was sixteen. You could be forgiven for thinking it a stroke of luck: preferential treatment by my mother's sister and an enormous advantage over the other pupils. Well, that impression could not be more wrong. From day one, perfection was expected of me. After all, I was the Reverend Mother's niece. I dared not let my mother down or bring disgrace on our family.

It's a shame she was not from Dad's side of the family, which would have been a different matter. But I can remember visiting my maternal grandmother, at the age of four or five, and finding her in bed, where my sister and I were summoned to see her. As we entered the bedroom, she rapped the floor with a heavy blackthorn stick and barked at us.

'You two... sit down and don't make a sound!' She was strictly of the old 'children should be seen and not heard' school. We were petrified and wracked our brains for what we had possibly done wrong. My lasting memory of this one and only visit was of her as a cold, uncaring, menacing woman. I think back on this encounter sometimes, and realise it is no wonder my mother could not show me love, never having received any sign of it herself.

I soon realised that this coveted scholarship was a millstone around my neck. It certainly did not turn out to be a privilege. I felt continually in a glaring spotlight, as if the nuns were hovering, waiting for me to step out of place so they could humiliate me – and preferably in front of onlookers.

As if that was not enough for a young child to contend with, my father accepted a post in England that coincided with my start at boarding school. The upshot was that my parents and siblings upped sticks and moved to England, leaving me with the nuns in Dublin and increasing my sense of loneliness and isolation. Mother always decided what was best for the family and, this time, it was moving to England for a better life. My greatest disappointment was that my parents decided they could not afford me to come home each holiday, and I so missed seeing my beloved father. And so, at the age of eight, I saw myself as completely and utterly abandoned.

Around the age of twelve, I woke in pain one night to find my sheet drenched in blood. Everyone was asleep, but my bed was right next to one of the two nuns who slept either end of the dormitory in case any child was sick during the night. I had never been told the facts of life so I could not work out what was happening. I was frightened and thought there must be something seriously amiss. I remember lying in my cubicle on my blood-soaked sheet, crying because I thought I was going to die. The nun in charge woke up, heard my sobs and pulled back the curtain between us. As soon as she noticed my sheet she reacted swiftly. *At last, someone to comfort me... send for help... explain.* But that wasn't her reaction at all! No, she reached over for her cane and beat me, just as my mother had when I spilled the milk on my way home from Purcells' farm. Even though it was so long ago, I still feel the caning I got from that nun, and ransacking my frightened brain for how I had misbehaved. When she was eventually satisfied with my punishment, she gave me an old rag to wear and told me not to wake the whole dormitory.

In the morning, I was sent to the sick bay, where Sister Eugene sat me down and quietly reassured me that I was not going to die. She explained that my body was changing from a child to a young woman, gave me some sanitary towels, and told me how and when to use them. I was almost melted with relief when she gave me a hug and told me not to worry – that she was always there if I was afraid or needed to talk. But even Sister Eugene's compassion was too little, too late. I look back at these women, my mother and the dormitory nun, and understand that they were not able to pass on love because they had never received any kindness in the first place.

After this incident I even more desperately longed to leave the convent and pestered my parents with letters asking them to let me come home, to live with my siblings who I hardly knew anymore. Finally, a whole year later, they agreed to me living in the family home. By then I had a sister aged twelve, one brother of eleven and two aged six and four. My last sibling was another sister, born when I was sixteen.

I told Mum and Dad that I wanted to take the 13+ exam to gain a place at a Croydon grammar school. Sure, it was another convent, but at least it was not a boarding school. They agreed, and I passed into my third and last school.

And all was going well in Croydon until one night in May when disaster struck. I had been revising for my final year exams and gone to bed early, when I was woken by my mother calling urgently up the stairs. Surely... *it's not morning already?* I thought. I rushed down to find Mum in the sitting room, with a priest. As soon as I came in, he asked me to kneel down.

'Why, Father?' I remember asking.

'Your father has died and we all need to pray for his soul,' he answered.

'No, Father, that can't be right. He wasn't sick!' It had to be a mistake.

'Brigid, I'm afraid your father had a heart attack… as he was leaving work.'

I stood like a statue, stuck to the ground - numb with disbelief. My world was turned upside down that night. I was heartbroken. I had lost my kind, loving father; the one steadfast person in my life. My greatest wish had been to make him proud of me, and it had been stolen in an instant.

How can life be this cruel? I asked myself. And then, more shockingly: *Why wasn't it, Mum?* My father had never hurt anyone in his life and was the kindest person I ever knew. I still feel the same about him today. The heartache remains as I write, and will be until the day I join him in the next world.

His death had significant consequences for me. It was the worst day of my life, but my new life after Daddy's death took me suddenly down a different path. I had been revising for my GCE exams and had every reason to expect an academic future, but it soon became clear that as the oldest of the six children, I was required to get a job and become the family breadwinner. No university for me then; that was put on hold.

I applied for a job in the Bank of England, which asked for five 'O' Levels (including Maths and English). I had to become a British citizen, sign the Official Secrets Act and pass an interview. It felt a tall order whilst in a state of shock and trying to come to terms with the absence of my wonderful Dad. Heartbroken as I was, I went onto automatic pilot and somehow steered through those months, although I will never know how.

Devastated as I was, I vowed that If I had children they would be loved and protected from such trauma, so that they could develop into compassionate and caring people.

Chapter 19

SAVING THE REEF

That evening brought our farewell dinner. After a swim, we returned to the Inlet restaurant where we came for my first meal here. It seemed like only yesterday, and I dined on a fish called the Red Emperor.

We were sad to say goodbye, but thanks to Brenda and Peter's generosity of spirit, the stay had showered me with a cascade of firsts. I learned to breathe and swim underwater, confidently, without panicking, just as I had learned the knack of breathing in bustling airports and wandering through unfamiliar crowds and cities. I had a truly fantastic and unforgettable introduction to Australia and couldn't find enough ways that night to thank Brenda for inviting me to share her birthday. I shall never forget my time in Port Douglas as long as I live.

Like a child at the end of a party, I was downhearted when my friends left me at the airport to board my flight to Brisbane. It was good to feel my feet firmly supported by Fred again, and to feel Ruby nudge snugly against my back, but I couldn't imagine Brisbane, or anywhere else, topping the last week. I revisited my prowess in and out of the water, and even on the dance floor, and felt indescribably lucky for the friendship and guidance that accompanied me through that whole world of adventures. I had been 'down under' in every sense.

Contemplations of my gratitude were interrupted by an announcement blaring over the public address system: 'The next flight to Brisbane will be at 6 p.m.' So, what happened to the three o'clock flight I was booked on? It had been cancelled, but no information was forthcoming.

Never mind, I suppose it could be worse. I decided. *I'll use the time to catch up on my travel blog.*

I rummaged around and hoiked my neglected diary from Ruby's deepest recess, immersed myself in my notes, and was oblivious to time passing.

In fact, my concentration felt rudely interrupted three hours later by a call to board a flight that would get me into Brisbane at seven o'clock.

My flight neighbour was an Indigenous Australian:

a striking, elegant woman who was at least six feet tall. Being actively curious when travelling alone means you get to engage with some interesting people.

We Irish tend to be sociable and it is quite usual for me to chat with strangers, so we got into conversation as fellow travellers. I put this openness down to the fact that the Irish have few enemies and have never invaded any other country. My Irish passport has proved an advantage wherever I've landed, and I'm frequently told by immigration control that their father or mother come from Ireland. I have always been made welcome. Perhaps it's 'the luck of the Irish', but I never have problems when presenting my passport for inspection or mentioning my nationality.

The statuesque woman next to me was attending a conference in Brisbane about the impact of global warming on the Great Barrier Reef. I was enthusiastic to hear what she had to say as the reef had left such a strong and emotional impression with me.

She was an authority on coral reefs, with senior responsibilities for the Great Barrier, and had attended the 2004 World Conference in Copenhagen on global warming. I was spellbound listening to her speak about the impact of humans, and began to feel quite guilty to be part of the human race contributing to its degradation. She opened my eyes to a fresh perspective of the need to act responsibly and protect the oceans' future. I would love to meet her again, having watched David Attenborough's *Blue Planet* with a new awareness, and to catch up on her present views on the condition of the reefs.

I felt privileged to have met her, and all because I was travelling alone.

I had watched Paul grow from babyhood into a lovely man who emigrated to Australia with his wife Linda and children, and recognised him the second I entered the Arrivals' Hall. His mother Margaret is a lifelong friend, and hearing that Brisbane was on my itinerary she naturally told Paul who invited me to stay. He greeted me with a great big smile and a bear hug – he hadn't changed at all.

Having heard such glowing reports of the Gold Coast, I planned a leisurely drive from Brisbane to Sydney to experience it myself, so I had pre-booked a hire car at the airport which would facilitate spontaneous stops and overnight stays anywhere I fancied en route. Paul was a godsend; he sorted out the paperwork then drove in front of me to his Brisbane suburb.

Linda came out to welcome us home. I loved catching up with their new lives, and meeting Cameron and Amy who had grown considerably since I had last seen them in England and did not remember me. Why would they?

Amy gave me the house tour and showed me the guest bedroom with en-suite. What a confident and self-assured girl she was. That evening we sat tranquilly on the terrace and celebrated my safe arrival with wine and beer, watching the children play in the secluded garden that backed onto woodland. After tea Paul supervised bedtime while Linda prepared dinner for us, over which they described their life here; it was considerably more laid back than it had been in England.

'Thank heaven for a bit of space to spread out in instead of being scrunched in hotel wardrobes,' said Ruby that evening. Fred shuffled around the wardrobe floor, which he now had all to himself, and settled down contentedly as I too stretched out and fell into a deep sleep.

I was welcomed into the next morning by the delicious smells of breakfast prepared by Paul. Linda explained she was not on strike but was a night owl, not much of a morning person.

That day, John, an old family friend, was coming

up from Sydney. We were planning on a spot of sightseeing before setting off together on my 900-kilometre drive down to Sydney. Linda and Paul offered him their other spare room so we could make an early start. It was a thoughtful idea that I was pleased to accept, as who knew when I would visit them again.

So, I drove into town to collect John from the station. Who was this John, anyway? I need to rewind ten years to a holiday in the Channel Islands.

I used to spend my long summer holidays with my mother and mother-in-law in a Jersey guesthouse where Sue was a permanent lodger and more like a companion to the owner. She immediately struck me as a lively and cheerful person, and she asked if I would like to play tennis with her. I told her I was dreadful at tennis but could hold my own at golf.

One day on the beach she introduced me to Joan, owner of a bar famously used in *Bergerac*, one of my favourite TV detectives, and she invited me to play at the golf club. As luck had it, we were the same shoe size, and her husband Ken had a spare set of clubs. All that remained was for me to beg permission from the two matriarchs to disappear for the afternoon. They seemed happy to be rid of me so they could pass a few hours putting the world to rights.

Our friendship blossomed, so that I regularly played golf with them each summer when I returned to Jersey. At the end of one visit, Joan and Ken invited an old friend to our, now customary, farewell dinner. They had grown up together in Liverpool, and even after John emigrated to Australia they stayed in touch.

That evening I was regaling John about how my daughter was off backpacking when she finished college, before settling into a job, and would be visiting Australia. He gave me his business card, promised to meet Siobhan at the airport, and invited her to stay at their family home until she found her feet.

I was delighted and, sure enough, Siobhan stayed in Sydney with John, his wife Jean and their three sons. Her three-day stay turned into three months, during which Siobhan became the daughter they'd never had. When she left John had told her, 'If you get married, I'm flying over to attend your wedding!' And he did.

So, it seemed natural when I was planning my trip that Siobhan suggested I contact John and Jean, which brought an immediate invitation to stay with them.

As the date grew closer John suggested he could meet me in Brisbane and help with the navigation and driving. It seemed a great offer and allayed some of my apprehension about being alone on this long road trip. *No matter how careful you are things can always go wrong,* I told myself. How right I was!

Chapter 20

A TEDIOUS TRAVELLING COMPANION

I was driving down the Gold Coast with a man I had only met twice. First, when we were introduced in Jersey and, second, when he flew into Ireland to attend my daughter's wedding. And now he was sitting next to me for a week-long drive down the Pacific coast. As he knew the route, he started off as my navigator. It felt pleasant having someone to talk to and I thought how accommodating it was of Jean to spare him, especially for someone she had never met. It didn't cross my mind that it was a bit of a risk. After all, what could possibly go wrong?

I had done my homework to familiarise myself with the route and the road was quiet, allowing me to enjoy the scrumptious scenery until John's voice vented from the passenger seat.

'Typical woman driver!'

'I beg your pardon?'

'Can't you keep your eyes on the road?'

I was taken aback. Where had that come from?

'Excuse me?' I bantered. 'Whose idea was it to join me on this road trip?' I was only half joking. 'Would you rather get out and walk?'

'Who does he think he is... God Almighty?' chirped up Ruby.

'Only teasing!' insisted John.

'Don't you think I'll get you home in one piece?'

Is he right? I wondered. *Maybe I shouldn't be checking out the scenery.* But we arrived safely at Glasshouse Mountain and I put it behind me.

'Fancy a hike to stretch our legs?' I asked.

'Count me out!' he replied. 'I don't own hiking boots... and I'm not keen on mountains anyway. I'll have a few beers in the tavern while you're on your hike.'

I was taken aback but recalibrated and headed enthusiastically for the mountain tracks.

'See you later then!' I waved.

'Actually, that's a relief... not having to put up with that miserable git,' chuntered Fred.

I told him to hush and not be unkind but to enjoy the walk, and after a nice breath of air we joined John in the café where I got talking to some geologists at the next table.

It wasn't hard to spot the signs that John was not the slightest bit interested in our conversation. What had happened to the companionable man I'd met in Jersey?

He was sulking about something. *Maybe he doesn't like me talking to other men?* I thought, and dismissed it.

We drove on to Noosa, north of the Glasshouse Mountains, a smart seaside place, upmarket and littered with boutique hotels, swish apartments and fine restaurants. I had pre-booked one of the cute boutique hotels near the surfing beach. But, oh dear, I had only booked one room because I was expecting to be travelling alone.

'That's alright. We can share!' said John, assuming I was happy to sleep in the same room – even the same bed.

'He's gotta be kidding, right?' asked Ruby.

Luckily, the receptionist interpreted the surprise on my face and found a handy cancellation. *Am I giving out the wrong vibes?* I questioned myself, feeling tangibly relieved. *Is it going to be this tricky all the way?* I hoped not.

Having dodged that bullet and wangled out of a delicate situation, I asked about the local food. She recommended a Thai restaurant, and I explained how much I had loved the food in Bangkok. She couldn't promise Bangkok standards but booked us in anyway. Feeling uncomfortable that John might think I was depending on him financially, I insisted we should go halves on this trip and, to my relief, he agreed. I very much wanted to maintain my independence right now.

With that sorted, I could enjoy my meal. John asked if I played golf and what my handicap was?

'Well, the main handicap is HIM!' whispered Ruby.

I gave her a gentle kick, and told him that I played off ten.

'Not bad for a woman.'

I just ignored it.

We cruised on down the coast, passing wide empty sandy beaches and a consistently dazzling blue-green sea. The only heavy traffic was in and out of Surfers' Paradise on the Gold Coast.

'Keep your eyes off the surfers and on the road, will you,' instructed my navigator.

'I reckon he's jealous of those fit bronzed blokes,' added Ruby.

I had to swallow his sarcasm because I had accepted his invitation to stay and was stuck with him.

'Look here, why don't you go in the back and leave me to do the driving?'

'Sounds alright.' To my surprise he agreed.

'The deal is you stop making negative comments... or, better still, go to sleep.'

'He's not sitting next me!' insisted an alarmed Ruby.

So, as he climbed into the rear seat, I told him to pass over my rucksack.

'Happy now you're up front, Ruby?' She was.

So now, I revved up the car for New Brighton. Brighton in Sussex is my home town, also by the sea, but this Brighton was not on the churning grey English Channel but north of the spectacular Byron Bay.

At Brenda's birthday party, I was invited to stay overnight in New Brighton with Pam and Graeme. On arrival, I had to explain that John had unexpectedly joined me so we'd find rooms in town, but Pam was quick to offer us her two guestrooms. The house was a magical place, with a terrace overlooking Byron Bay beach and its surfers. Graeme cooked king prawns, and we tucked into salads and wine on their peaceful deck watching the ocean roll in and out.

Later, we walked along the beach and swam in the inlet. it proved to be a much-needed recuperative break on our journey. As we strolled, Pam quizzed me about my touring companion, which gave me the opportunity to confide that it felt a big mistake but that it was too late to do anything about it.

We showered and recharged our batteries before going for pizza in the village where a lively band was creating a great atmosphere for people gathered in the square. It felt a perfect way to wind up what could have gone down as a difficult day.

The next day we had agreed to visit John's good friend who lived in the neighbourhood. So, we did. Marcus was delighted to see him but may have wondered who I was. I'm not sure what John told him about our setup, but he gave me a few bemused smiles.

Marcus booked us rooms in town before taking us to meet his six-week-old baby and very welcoming and bubbly young wife. He seemed to have started a family late in life, being in his mid-sixties while she was about thirty but in spite of the age difference, they seemed happy and certainly doted on their beautiful baby. It showed me that sometimes age does not matter and wished them well in bringing up their daughter.

What had started as a frisson of tension between John and me, was becoming more of a tremor. The ever-present implication was that he was doing me a big favour, and its effect was to undermine my confidence as if I were incapable of travelling alone. It was no good closing the door after the horse had bolted though. We were at a point of no return, so I fixed on my brave face and resolved to enjoy every beautiful place along the way.

A word of warning to women on the road as I was. Don't do as I did and imagine a road trip with Prince Charming but get landed with a frog.

'To be honest, that sounds a bit froggist,' Ruby called me out. 'It's insulting to amphibia.'

You get the gist, I'm sure. It was quite a learning curve to realise, this late in life, that not all men are like Michael who treated all women with the utmost courtesy, kindness and respect. I consoled myself knowing his wife would soon be there for support. Focusing on that made it easier to keep my cool and not react to John's taunts.

Our guesthouse at Brooms Head was in a national park; a stunning four-star bed and breakfast owned by a lovely couple from New Zealand and, as the season had not started, we had the place to ourselves.

Then we were heading south, through Port Macquarie to Laurieton, where we took a cottage owned by another of John's friends.

'Aren't you worried about being in a cottage with him?' checked Ruby.

'No, of course not – I'm not *completely* gullible, you know!' But the first thing I did was to test if my bedroom door could be locked. It could.

I kept a distance, without being rude, and was left to do my own thing because John spent his time reading on the patio. We found a local restaurant each night for dinner, as I really couldn't face a romantic candle-lit meal in the cottage with Romeo; anyway, I try to avoid shopping, cooking or cleaning on holiday.

It was relaxing to stay put for a couple of days and take daily swims among the dolphins, which was heaven! Laurieton is a delightful spot with lakes, rivers, mountains, sandy beaches and sea, all on the doorstep. Once there were only four people on the sands, which seemed like my own private beach. They told me that only the locals used this beach... but, we found it!

I was building up an enviable tan, though being fair skinned I made my way through lots of high-factor sunscreen and always wore a hat. The sun was so much hotter here and I could not possibly lie in it for long stretches without ending up like a cooked lobster. It was disappointing that my co-pilot was not more affable company, but I hoped his mood would improve back home in Sydney.

Blue Haven was our next port of call, where we met up with yet more of Brenda's friends, Tony and Angie. We had lunch at their house and had intended to stay overnight, but by now I was keen to put some road under the tyres and even John suggested we go straight to his place in Cronulla, South Sydney. That was music to my ears. *No more chauffeuring – yippee!*

We finally reached Cronulla where John gave me a brief guided tour of the cafés and sandy beaches, but there was no sign of Jean. He didn't elucidate, but showed me to a pretty en-suite guest room, which was caringly designed with all amenities and a feminine touch.

'Where's your wife then, John?' I had to ask the question.

And then it all came out. Apparently, they did not live together anymore, but he had not felt it relevant to tell me.

'See? I told you something was dodgy,' said Ruby.

Jean had only moved ten minutes away and they were amicable for the sake of their children and the grandchildren.

'How come you never mentioned it?' I asked.

'What difference does it make?' he answered. 'Use the house as a base. Here's a key... just come and go as you like.'

I felt uncomfortably wedged between a rock and a hard place. I had no idea that I would need a contingency plan. There was nothing I could do that evening and, anyway, I was too tired and surprised to say any more.

I was thankful to go out for dinner, there being no food in the house.

'Didn't know what you'd like,' he explained. 'So, I played safe and didn't get anything in.'

I was too dazed to care by now so just went along with his line of reasoning.

It was an anticlimax compared to the warmth and hospitality I had received so far. Michael wasn't far away though. I heard him quietly reassuring me, 'Take it one day at a time, girl.' I geared up to be positive, not let this disappointment define my visit to Sydney. *The whole city's waiting for you tomorrow,* I reminded myself. *You're doing fine... just keep stepping out.*

Chapter 21

TUBOWGULE

Where the knowledge waters meet

So, John had been a free agent to meet me in Brisbane and drive down the Pacific Coast. Now I felt trapped and wanted out. I found it hard to read the actual situation, but knew I was deeply shaken up and disappointed at being misled. *Do I stay or move on? But, where to?*

I got up void of my usual zest next day, still drained by the difficult drive but also fazed by feelings of deception and betrayal. John must have talked to Jean by the time I rallied for coffee, as she had invited us over for lunch.

I had mixed emotions about meeting her; I dreaded what she would think of me having spent a week with John on the road, and now staying in their house. But I needn't have worried because she straightaway made me very welcome. Jean is a fit slender woman with a lovely temperament. I speculated on why they had split up, but also questioned what she had seen in him in the first place. I dared to assume they had stayed together because of the boys. Two of their sons joined us for lunch, and I swept away crazy thoughts that they were checking me out as a stepmother. Jean asked about my plans and offered her local know-how if I needed it. I liked her and was settling down into feeling more secure. By this time, I think she had formed her own opinion about me.

She's much too good for him, I thought.

'Waste of space!' piped up Ruby.

If I had known what I now know, I would have been more tolerant of John's behaviour and more compassionate towards him and Jean, but he hadn't felt it necessary to confide in me, so there was no chance of my understanding their situation. Not knowing each other well enough meant maybe he was unable to open up to me and we got off to a dreadful start. I later learned that their son had died in a quad bike accident that summer, leaving behind his young wife and six-month old baby. It was about to be a very rough Christmas.

But I didn't know, and I had to pick up some city guides and return the hire car to Sydney airport. We swung by the supermarket, where John left me drifting without a word and did the shopping without checking my preferences, which at the time confirmed my impression of him as a born chauvinist. He went off for some beers at his surf club that evening, and I was tremendously pleased to have some 'me time' in which to recuperate.

The following evening his friend Judy invited us to the yacht club for dinner. I was fascinated to guess what kind of woman she'd be: timid, shy and compliant...? Or maybe the total opposite, loud, brash and self-assured? I had only experienced John as arrogant, so was uneasy about what friends he would attract.

For me, two iconic landmarks were synonymous with Sydney: I simply had to climb up Sydney Harbour Bridge and attend a performance at the Sydney Opera House. I knew I'd be spending as little time as possible at John's, and caught the train from Cronulla into Sydney Central early each day. Circular Quay is the main hub for international cruise ships, buses, taxis and trains. My friend Alice, a frequent visitor to her sister in Australia, had mentioned eight different boat trips: Taronga Zoo, Watson's Bay, Manly, Paramatta, Close Bay, Cockatoo Island, Balmain, Cremone Point and Mossman Bay. Each route, run by Sydney Ferries, was wrapped around sightseeing walks during the journey. They certainly kept me entertained, and by the time I left for New Zealand I had taken every ferry trip from the harbour. They were among the best bargains I found, and I treated myself to a celebratory coffee and pastry on the promenade overlooking the harbour to mark each return.

Armed with information, I came back to Cronulla to get ready for dinner with Judy. We met her at the yacht club and had a lovely meal looking over the harbour. Once again, the fish was fresh and full of flavour. Judy was charming, although she seemed a private person. And John behaved like a perfect gentleman, which made me question his previous behaviour.

'How come you didn't get the upmarket treatment?' said Ruby.

'No chemistry there,' I told her. 'It must be me.'

As we left, Judy offered to pick me up for ten o'clock Mass next morning, and after church she dropped me off for the train into Sydney, where I was meeting Tom and Patricia for our promised lunch trip to Doyle's, which I knew to be world famous for its Sydney Rock oysters. I had accepted in Port Douglas and was certainly not going to pass it up.

They had booked a perfect outside table, looking onto Watson's Bay. I tasted my first rock oysters and snapper fillets and washed them down with a crisp and fruity *Margaret River* Sauvignon Blanc. As a gentle aid to digestion, we walked along the headland, from where the Sydney to Hobart Yacht Race would be leaving on Boxing Day. I made a vow to seize the day and be standing right there for the start of the race.

Day after day I found myself not quite believing the extraordinary things I was doing, how I was visiting places I had only dreamed of. And day after day reaffirmed to me how much Michael would have enjoyed being by my side. I was continuing to feel the deepest sadness that he had been taken from me, missed him at so many moments, and often felt bereft that we were not experiencing these times together.

I started Monday by putting my foot in it again with John.

'Is there any fresh coffee, John?'

You'd think I had asked for the sun, moon and

stars!

'You're pretty high maintenance, aren't you?' he snapped. 'Do you think it's a five-star hotel?'

Well, that put me in my place.

'There's a jar of Nescafé right in front of your nose,' he barked.

Although peeved, when John and Jean invited me along to visit their daughter-in-law and grandchildren on the Wednesday, I accepted.

In the meantime, and quite out of the blue I got a call from Myfanwy's son, Simon, saying that his mother had arrived in Sydney and wanted us to meet up. I was delighted to have a day free of engagements and excited about seeing her again, so next day I met them at the Art Gallery of New South Wales, in The Domain.

Myfanwy is part of our gang who all took early retirement on the same day, when we made a pact to keep in regular touch and always be there for each other. How prophetic this promise turned out when I was widowed because I badly needed someone to have my back. My fellow workers have kept me going in many ways and I am always there for them. I would be lost without them. 'Old friends are the best friends' has proved indisputable in my life.

So, I met Myfanwy when I was teaching computerised accounting and was based in the Computer Department staff room at the only desk available, which was next to her. We discovered mutual interests in our love of opera, classical music and theatre, and over the years we have been to some big opera houses together. Another mutual connection was the Bank of England where her husband spent his working life and which was my first job when I left school.

Now, she and Anthony were in town to spend Christmas and New Year with Simon, his wife Alison and son Liam. I wondered if we could manage an opera or classical concert together while she was here.

After a hearty welcome and some lunch, Simon headed off for a meeting, leaving Myfanwy and me to wander around the Pissarro exhibition before moving on to an illuminating collection of Asian and Aboriginal artwork.

For thousands of years, before 1770 and the arrival of Lieutenant James Cook and his crew, Northern Sydney was home to diverse Indigenous Aboriginal clans. Around 750,000 Indigenous Australians were recorded as living here harmoniously, even back in 1788. Now they comprise just over 3% of the population. They did not build fences because they lived in one area for a few weeks before moving on to find fresh food and bush medicine. Being nomadic by nature, their culture was one of self-sufficiency and resourcefulness.

Here, along the shores of Sydney, they fished, hunted and harvested food from the surrounding area. The place where Sydney Opera House now stands was named *Tubowgule*, 'where the knowledge waters meet'. Life went on as it had for thousands of years until Cook arrived from England, shortly followed by the First Fleet who had been ordered to establish a penal colony and seize Australian lands for European settlement. No negotiation occurred, nor was consent obtained from the Aboriginal tribes, but these actions sealed the decline of their lifestyle and heritage. White settlers depleted the fish, reduced the kangaroo population, cleared the land and polluted the water. As if that was not enough devastation, they brought with them smallpox, syphilis and influenza. In less than a year, over half the Aboriginal people in the Sydney area had died from smallpox.

The coastal regions, once alive with dynamic Aboriginal clans, were now silent. Indigenous people were found dead and dying in caves and on the beaches. In the shortest time, European intruders destroyed a way of life that had outlasted their own history by tens of thousands of years. I felt a confused mixture of sorrow and anger as I learned their stories and studied their art, and I had to deal with feelings of shame towards my European heritage. By the time we left this magnificent gallery, I was subdued and thoughtful. Later, exploring the Sydney suburbs and caves, I came across many Aboriginal carvings, still visible after hundreds of years due to non-exposure to sunlight.

Simon collected us for dinner with his wife, Alison and little Liam. He turned out to be a fantastic cook who obviously enjoyed conjuring up the family meals. I had yet another new fish, new to me anyway. Blue Cod is nothing like British cod from the North Sea or Atlantic. For one thing it was tastier. We had a starter of Sydney Rock oysters, and I was quite blasé about them, having tasted them the previous day at Doyle's!

Myfanwy and I met up again next day, at the botanical gardens, which proved a really *cool* place to be. I mean it! The temperature was extremely comfortable as we strolled under the unfamiliar antipodean trees. Afterwards, we booked tickets for the Christmas Carols Concert at the Opera House, and for the new opera season in January. There were upcoming productions of *Falstaff*, and *L'elisir d'amore*, but I chose *Madame Butterfly*. Having planned those outings, we relaxed together over coffee on the Opera House terrace, just watching the boats go by. It was perfect. Sydney is breathtaking.

Back at Simon and Alison's, Simon poured me a heavy-handed Bombay Sapphire and tonic! He makes a mean cocktail, and I don't mean stingy! Myfanwy and I were our usual easy company, and she knew Sydney inside out! After dinner Simon showed me the bus stop because, just like London, public transport across Sydney is a lot easier than using a car.

The next day John, Jean and I set off for Goulburn to visit their family - as arranged. It was only now, on the way there, that they told me how their son had been killed that summer while leading a trip into the outback when his quad bike hit the root of an old tree and he was catapulted out as it smashed against the tree trunk. They were told he died instantly, at thirty-two years old, leaving his wife, a three-year old and a baby.

The wife's one and only comfort was that her parents and siblings lived close by, and they were a tight-knit family. Despite their own grief and shock, they focused on supporting her through the days, helping her and each other through the despair. I could barely imagine what this young widow must be going through, with no soulmate to help her raise their young children or keep her warm in bed. I was fortunate in that my children were adults when their father died. They somehow managed to comfort and console me.

Now, suddenly, I realised that John and Jean's relationship issues were not straightforward. Their hearts were heavily weighed down and their boy must have been always uppermost in their minds. This imminent Christmas was going to be complicated for all of them.

In touching their daughter-in-law's sorrow, I became painfully aware of my own emptiness this Christmas, without my husband or children to share it with? I grew despondent at not having Michael with me, and knowing I would never enjoy his company or wicked sense of humour again. My children seemed even further away than ever before.

At next day's carol concert, with Myfanwy and Alison, I cried my eyes out in empathy with the young widow I had taken in my arms and tried to console yesterday, unable to rid my mind of our respective Christmas festivities without our husbands. Michael attended a carol service with me every year and, without fail, I teased him for singing off key. The more I tried to shut him up the worse he got – just to wind me up! His thoughtful planning had brought me here to sing carols in this magnificent venue, and I longed for him to be singing off key once more. I truly appreciated Myfanwy, who tried so hard to comfort me, but was emotionally exhausted by the end of the service.

A trip to the Christmas shops lifted my spirits. It was the best possible treat for Alison as she could browse and shop without being distracted by baby Liam. Simon came up trumps with a pan of fresh mussels for us and I had bought some wine for dinner. It had been a full-on day; a bittersweet blend of delight, wretchedness and tears. I took the train back to Cronulla in a sombre reflective mood and was glad to find John out as I did not want to talk. I longed to sleep as soundly as I could, to block out my grief.

I had promised Michael to take one day at a time, so on Friday morning I chivvied myself into action: *Buck up Brigid and move on.*

John suggested a game of golf with his regular group and I seized the opportunity.

'Go on, show him what you're made of, girl!' encouraged Ruby.

'Don't you worry... I won't be going easy on them,' I promised her.

Fourteen were playing in their weekly competition, which I was not eligible to join, but I could enter the 'par threes' competition' for nearest the pin, provided I put my contribution in the kitty. I hoped it would shift yesterday's melancholy.

Out on the course, the group behind us was enjoying some lively banter and throwing comments at John. I had an awkward feeling that I was the butt of their jokes, and wondered if some of the remarks I overheard were directed at my friendship with him. 'Nudge, nudge! Wink, wink!' Sometimes one has a sixth sense about these things.

'In his dreams...' stage-whispered Ruby from the buggy.

Everyone met at the surf club that evening to hear the results announced, so I went along and played gooseberry. I had managed to win nearest the pin on two of the par threes and was awarded $30 for that achievement. I quickly put the money behind the bar as my contribution to the drinks' kitty.

Chapter 22

CHRISTMAS BLUES

It was Christmas Eve, poignant with heartache and expectations. Last night I left John's friends with the clear message that I was not in a relationship with him, but I had an inkling that they didn't believe me.

I hung my washing out to dry in the sunshine. I don't use tumble dryers, if I have the choice, preferring the fresh air whenever possible. We breakfasted, and John proposed taking the ferry from Cronulla to Bundeena then walking around the headland.

Where had this idea come from? It seemed out of the blue as we had not mentioned ferry trips. Perhaps he noticed my boat trip leaflets hanging about? Anyway, Christmas was around the corner and I wanted to respond graciously, with charity and good spirits. After all my feelings paled into insignificance when I think of him losing his son. Their family Christmas without their boy was going to be very distressing – it would bring up all sorts of emotions that I could strongly understand.

The ferry crew knew many of the people on board. They were obviously regulars and behaving like an extended family! The banter was contagious, and I loved being out on the bay with no heavy swell or choppy seas, just a fair breeze blowing. A breath of fresh air for Christmas Eve.

We sailed out into Gunnamatta Bay towards Port Hacking with its old stately homes and grand gardens that sloped graciously down to the shoreline. These desirable properties boasted the most stunning location. When we reached shore, I saw that they had a 360-degree uninterrupted view of Sydney. Wow! It made me gasp.

We landed at Bundeena, gateway to the Royal National Park, with its coastal cliffs and quiet beaches. It was already 37 degrees and far too hot to be out in the sun so we found a pretty café for lunch, from where we admired the eucalyptus-rich bushland, distant landmarks, and the brightly-coloured birds. Bundeena is one of Sydney's hidden treasures. It turned out to be an unexpected and relaxing jaunt, still like a family outing, with a friendly crew who were clearly being paid for a job they enjoyed.

Time whizzed by, and we headed back to Cronulla where Jean and I wanted to attend the Children's Christmas Mass. John dropped me off and went to meet friends at the surf club.

The Mass was bursting at the seams with kids of all ages and sizes who sang festive carols with youthful zeal. It seemed a thriving community, with plenty of young mums and dads making for an enthusiastic and inclusive atmosphere.

I felt sharper pangs of nostalgia watching them. There are certain occasions when being with your own children or grandchildren feels particularly precious, and this children's Mass was one of them. I was in a crowded church, but alone. I couldn't afford to be gloomy or downhearted though as I had a long road ahead, and I pulled myself up sharply. I was not even halfway through my journey.

I went back for dinner with Jean. We both knew that if there was ever a time, we needed each other's company, it was now. In our mutual bereavements we could offer mutual comfort and companionship.

I awoke fragile and subdued on Christmas morning. I don't think it crossed John's mind to wonder what it felt like for me to be away from my family. He too had suffered an outstanding loss and was caught up in his own grief. Today, of all days, I wanted to show charity and care towards him and his family. I had not looked forward to being just the two of us in his soulless home but Jean had invited us over for the day. Their sons, Mark and John, were with her when we arrived. Robert was undeniably there in spirit, and his wife and children came for Christmas dinner.

In the afternoon we played the card game, UNO. I hadn't played it before but soon got the hang of it and we all had fun. I made a mental note to teach it to my grandchildren. After sharing a traditional evening dinner, we watched Christmas programmes for a while. I was gratified to be part of this difficult family holiday, but I wanted to get back to John's by ten because my own children were phoning and I wouldn't miss their calls for anything. It was so soothing to hear their voices wishing me a happy Christmas and asking for stories about my trip. Catherine reminded me that she was coming to meet me in New Zealand in February (as if I could forget!). It was just around the turn of the year now.

I missed them all and fought back my tears so as not to worry them. When I came off the phone I was in an emotional state and prepared to settle down in my room and mull over the day.

I was on my way up to bed when John came out with a very gauche comment.

'I know what bra size you are!' he said, quite pleased with himself.

'I beg your pardon?'

I thought I had misheard him. But he repeated himself, and went on to announce the size! I was flabbergasted.

'You're sick, John. You wouldn't dare say that if Michael was here.'

'Well, he's not. Is he?' he taunted.

I was so shocked that Christmas Day was ending like this that I burst into tears and ran into my room.

'What's up?' asked Ruby.

'She's had too much to drink,' said Fred, from the cupboard.

'No, she's upset that she's stuck with us,' Ruby added.

'Stop it both of you,' I said. 'Of course, it's not you.' And I told them what had happened.

'Oh, that's creepy,' said Ruby. 'Why don't you call your friend, Myf... what's-her-name?'

Even though I was flustered I rang Myfanwy and told her what John had said.

'Don't stay there with that man, Brigid,' she said. 'Lock your bedroom door, pack your things, and take a train into Sydney Central first thing in the morning. Simon will collect you.'

Next thing I knew, John was knocking on the door and asking me to come out.

'What's wrong with you? Can't you take a joke?'

I managed to spit out that it was not my idea of a joke, said a firm goodnight, and cried myself to sleep – thinking of my children.

When Fred and I emerged with Ruby on Boxing Day, he asked where I was off to, and I told him that I was visiting the Hunter Valley vineyards with a friend.

'Surely, you won't need all your clothes?' he quizzed.

'You know what women are like... they can't make up their minds what to wear, can they? Simpler to pack them all,' I retorted, playing his own game back at him.

He bought that story, not that I cared. I had no intention of spelling out that I was not coming back. He ran me to the station, and I never set foot in his house or wished to see him again. It felt a desolate way to end what had been a supportive Christmas Day, and any charitable feelings had flown out the window.

Simon met my train. Myfanwy and I had arranged to meet to see the Sydney to Hobart Yacht Race, which made the move less dramatic. Given the change of plan, the whole family tagged along to watch the start of the race. I left Ruby in a locker at the station.

'You will come back for me, won't you?' she asked.

'You're my friend now more than ever, Ruby,' I answered.

We caught the ferry to Taronga Zoo, where we watched the yachts sail from the harbour and far out to sea before then visiting the animals to keep baby Liam interested and active. It was another scorching day and we were glad to get back to an air-conditioned house. I was so relieved to be with Myfanwy's family, and away from John's awkwardness and innuendos. A weight was lifted off my shoulders when Alison told me to stay as long as I wanted.

That evening, Myfanwy suggested I ring John to be clear that I was not going back. I was not looking forward to a confrontation, but it had to be done, and I told him I had not appreciated his crude remarks.

'Well, suit yourself!' was his last throw-away before hanging up. That was the last time we spoke.

Chapter 23

ALONE IN A CROWD

My friend Alice has spent a lot of time in Australia and recommended the ferry from Circular Quay to Manly for the 10k Manly to Spithead coastal walk. What she didn't add was that it's not a walk – it's a serious hike! – but it was a festive treat for Fred, to stride out over secluded sandy beaches and through fabulous scenery in Balgowlah Heights nature reserve.

Early on, some fellow hikers stopped on the trail to chat.

'Make sure to check out the Aboriginal engravings near Castle Rock beach,' they insisted. 'Just slip a few metres off the trail to the exposed rock shelf... you'll see them high up on the rock.'

If we hadn't crossed paths I would probably have stayed on the main track and not laid eyes on those ancient carvings. Carved by the local Cammeraygal tribe, the engravings include fish, kangaroo, a whale, an emu, and something like footprints. The latter may just be natural indents in the rock platform, but have been dubbed 'ghost' footprints. Some are encased in wood surrounds to stop hikers walking on them, or desecrating them, as they are sacred. It certainly pays to chat with fellow hikers or I'd never have spotted the detour.

Another diversion led me to some heritage-listed fishing huts built during the Great Depression of 1923. They are pretty well maintained considering they are perched on the rocks and pounded by the elements. It made me appreciate organisations like the Heritage Trust who preserve these unique historical monuments.

Parts of that four-hour walk were challenging, but I rested, took pictures, admired the landscape and dipped down to headlands along the way. Fred had a whale of a time clambering over rough terrain and weaving through bush and scrubland. By the time we reached Spit Bridge we were pretty weary, but pleased with ourselves.

Would I do it again? Absolutely! It was fantastic and magical – especially the bush section, with the engravings.

All at once it was New Year's Eve, and I went

to Sydney Fish Market with Simon to choose a selection of fish for our New Year's celebration. What a place! It was a flurry of chefs and restauranteurs, rubbing shoulders with the general public, not unlike London's Billingsgate Fish Market.

We planned a picnic in Centennial Park, from where we could watch the fireworks display over the Sydney Harbour Bridge, and set off early to bag a first-class vantage point. Everyone around us was in good spirits and behaving themselves too. By the time the fireworks burst into life, thousands of people were crammed onto the small stretch of land, watching a beating red heart on the Sydney Bridge with a waterfall of fireworks cascading behind it. As the countdown to midnight began, an intense loneliness crept over me. No Michael. And, as much as I loved being there with my dear friends, they could not replace my loving family. I felt solitary in the midst of thousands of cheering happy people, all hugging and kissing. *This is not how it was meant to be.*

The Aussies certainly know how to put on a show and to party, and this was the perfect venue. Under different circumstances I would have thought *wow! Wow! WOW!* But here I was, without that most important person in my life. *How come I feel lonely in such a joyful crowd?* I thought. Yes, it happens. *Life's a bitch!*

'Happy New Year, Ruby. And to you, Fred,' I said. 'We're entering our second year together as a team!'

They didn't quite get it, but seemed pleased.

Myfanwy and Anthony were off home to London, but I was welcomed to use the young people's home as a base while I went off gallivanting. I could not have wished for anything more than knowing I had this warm family to return to. I was loath to say goodbye to Myfanwy, but promised to keep in touch on my journey and meet again soon, in England.

Chapter 24

GOLF IN THE BLUE MOUNTAINS

Before I left home, my golfing friend Angie told me that I absolutely *must* visit the Blue Mountains. Her friend Kerrie lived in Leura, the main town in the Blue Mountains National Park, and it turned out that she had a cottage that she rented out, and which I could use as a base while up there.

So, I boarded the train for the two-hour trip west to Kerrie's cottage at the top of the Blue Mountains. It was a pretty journey, with the train climbing upwards most of the time, and I felt the temperature drop as we climbed higher and made our way inland.

The mountains are called 'blue' because warmth causes the eucalyptus leaves to release their oils into the air, creating a blue haze. If you hear that question on *Mastermind* you will now know the answer! So much for squirrelling away general knowledge – but I never did stop being excited by what I found out on my travels.

A bustle of people got off at Leura and I peered through the throng trying to work out who might look like a 'Kerrie'. It hadn't crossed my mind to ask for a photo, or what she would be wearing. Was she tall or short? Hair colour? Glasses? I was about to phone her when a voice in my ear said, 'You must be Brigid!' I breathed a sigh of relief at her smiling face.

Indeed, it was Kerrie, and we bonded immediately. We drove to her peacefully situated cottage, which had everything I needed including all the basics for a healthy breakfast next morning. I was delighted not to have to go food shopping immediately. On the coffee table Kerrie had left information leaflets about trips I might enjoy.

'This is going to be fun,' said Ruby.

'Yep, I think you're probably right,' I agreed.

Once settled in I wanted to stretch my legs. It was only a ten-minute walk into Leura town centre, so I thought, *why not check out the locals!* Leura was such a pretty little place, high on a plateau at the entrance to the peaks. No wonder so many hikers got off the train with me. Leura Mall was lined with cherry trees, boutiques, restaurants, coffee shops, galleries, and an enchanting toy and railway museum for adults as well as children.

It was still early afternoon so, after a snack, I took a train to Katoomba, the region's federal capital. It was only one stop. In the tourist office they suggested a two-day voucher for a hop-on hop-off bus tour that offered guided commentary on beauty spots in the mountains. I had not done much prior reading so this was music to my ears.

I entered the cottage that evening with a spring in my step, and found a note from Kerrie on the mat inviting me out for a Chinese meal that evening. Of course, I was delighted to accept and thoroughly relaxed with her friends and Geoffrey, her husband, who kept us in high spirits with his wicked sense of humour! Before saying goodnight, Kerrie asked if I felt like a game of golf the next day. Angie must have told her I was keen.

Coincidentally, she too was Ladies Captain that year, so, once again, I was in esteemed company. It must look as if I have a 'thing' about playing with lady captains around the world. I promise you it just turned out that way. One acquaintance leads to another in a network of friends, I suppose.

Kerrie called next morning with a spare set of clubs and shoes. The scenic backdrop of this course was exceptional – an exhilarating setting. Even if my golf had been rubbish, I would still have lapped up the Blue Mountains scenery and the outlook would have compensated. As it was, I managed to acquit myself quite respectably.

After our game we lunched with Jennie, the Ladies President. No lunching with common or garden members for me! Then, as it was a perfect clear afternoon to see the magnificent views from Blackheath and Mount Victoria, Kerrie took me on a tour. We stopped for a cooling drink at Blackheath Golf Club, which is affiliated with the Royal Blackheath Golf Club in South London and where my special claim to fame was, years ago, winning their Centenary Cup. It is one of the oldest in the UK, and has reciprocal arrangements with its Leura 'twin', so I promised Kerrie to play her there one day. Another instance of feeling how small the world is.

I lay in the cottage that night feeling deep gratitude to my friend back home. *Angie, you're a star. I can't thank you enough for introducing me to Kerrie, this cottage and the Blue Mountains.*

I'd planned a bus outing, but my excitement was short-lived as when I woke up it was raining cats and dogs and visibility was practically nil through an impenetrable mist. What a bummer. It pelted down for the whole day, which meant no mountain train, sky ride or cable car for me. At least the hop-on hop-off bus tour voucher was flexible so I could use that another time. The weather hung on the next day too, but at least there was a break in the news if not the weather. Kerrie's friend invited me to their barbecue. Two men braved the elements and organised the barbie (please note the local lingo!). They did a great job, and a friendly company of fourteen tucked into it with gusto. So, despite the mountain mists and rain, I was not disappointed. Kerrie and Geoffrey treated me like family, and to this day we still exchange Christmas cards and newsletters.

I was not leaving until the following evening, and wanted to leave with a special memory of the Blue Mountains in case I didn't make it back. Kerrie came up with a perfect hike that fitted my schedule and left me with happy thoughts of my time in Leura, then dropped me at the station where I popped Ruby into a locker.

'Not again!' she protested. 'How come he's your favourite – every time?' She had a point, but I couldn't cart her up the hiking trails.

With my guided-walk information to hand, and even though it was cloudy, I took a well-signposted trail at the edge of town towards Leura Cascades, taking in the plentiful lookout points, waterfalls and peaks that offered a world-class show.

The cascades were the icing on the cake. They were a tucked-away gem, even though they were close to town. If I returned for a day trip, I would choose to walk beside the Leura Cascades – an easy-to-follow path, yet no crowds. I felt uplifted by the tranquility that reigned in spite of the resounding crash of waterfall torrents!

Ruby practically threw herself out of the locker. 'Don't do that again!' she told me. 'I'm gonna have your back in future.'

I felt sad boarding the return train, even though I was heading into sunnier weather, but the tourist office confirmed there was no expiry date on my bus voucher so I had a great excuse to come back. It was an education to realise how different mountain weather can be, even though it's only a two-hour ride from Sydney.

I already missed Myfanwy, who had been so supportive during that vulnerable time. The whole family made my transition to their home from John's seamless. I slept deeply, rejuvenated by gallons of mountain air, which was just what I needed to be bright-eyed and bushy-tailed for another busy day.

Darling Harbour here I come!

Chapter 25

THE HISTORY OF SYDNEY

This morning was strange on a number of counts. Firstly, I missed the waft of eucalyptus in the air, and then the stillness of no traffic. Finally, I missed my first cup of coffee with Myfanwy who was now on the other side of the world. On the plus side, I was with her charismatic son, his cheerful wife and the mischievous Liam. I allocated the morning to finding out what Darling Harbour had to offer.

Historically, Darling Harbour was named after Lieutenant-General Ralph Darling who was born in Dublin, Ireland, and became Governor of New South Wales from 1825–1831, and named this part of Sydney's commercial port after himself! He was from a family of British landed gentry who purloined vast Irish estates, but discussing this phenomenon would need an entire book on the politics of Ireland.

There was plenty to do so I was beset with choices, which I narrowed down to the Chinese Garden of Friendship, the Maritime Museum, and Paddy's Market.

The Chinese gardens mirror Sydney's strong Chinese culture and are modelled on private gardens of the Ming dynasty. I had never encountered such bewitchingly-shaped trees and plants, the horticulturalists' skillful topiary making them like works of origami. The ponds were full of Koi carp, and the design, based on Chinese principles of auspicious positioning for good energy, creates an oasis of peace. I listened to the waterfalls flowing over rocks into ponds, so close to a vibrant urban community.

Leaving the gardens behind me, I was hit by a wall of noise from the bustling Paddy's Market. I wandered this eclectic flea market; threaded between fruit, vegetable or fish stalls; browsed trinkets, clothes, shoes, old furniture. You name it – it was there. Being a 'Paddy', I was naturally curious about its origins.

Paddy's Market goes back to 1834 when it was set up by the next Governor of New South Wales, Richard Bourke, who, like Darling, was a Dublin-born British Army officer. It was based on a similar market in Liverpool, England, and Bourke courted the popularity with the locals by permitting it to trade until ten at night.

Next, were the naval ships at the Maritime Museum; in particular, a replica of Captain Cook's ship *Endeavour* and the destroyer HMS *Vampire* that fought against Japan during WWII. I get seasick just watching them on water, but here at the museum I was not struck down and learned that Captain Cook landed in Botany Bay in April 1770 and instantly claimed New South Wales for the British Crown.

At home, I regaled Simon and Alison about my educational day. Did they know who Darling Harbour was named after? No. Did they know how Paddy's Market originated? No. Well, we had a history lesson over the dinner table and the phrase 'singing for her supper' came to mind, or, in this case, I gave a history lesson for my supper.

Did I think, in my wildest dreams that, since November, I could have metamorphosed from that petrified insect who landed in Hong Kong, clamouring for the next plane home? I remember standing in the baggage reclaim area, paralyzed with fear and riveted to the ground with anxiety. I'm so grateful I plucked up enough courage to keep going. Sydney had captivated me, cocooned me, and I left some of my heart there. It ticked so many boxes to help me evolve, and I had only seen a fraction so far!

Simon and Alison had coddled me quite intensively, so now I had fully spread my wings I offered them a day's personal time by suggesting I look after Liam. It went down well and they launched into planning some quality time together. My good deed for the week!

I took Liam for a long outing to the park where he watched me feeding the ducks, after which I bought some new tee-shirts, and we arrived home in time for lunch. While he slept that evening, I uploaded my travel pictures into folders and burnt them onto disks. It was a laborious task and long overdue. Once up to date, I had dinner with a glass of wine and watched *Under the Tuscan Sun*, a feel-good film starring Maggie Smith and Ronnie Barker. I was benefitting from time to switch off instead of rushing around. It felt important to have time out from cramming as much as possible into every day. As I sunk into the sofa, I told myself, *I really should do it more often.*

Mum and Dad came home bubbling with excitement about their day: strolling the city, taking in an exhibition at Sydney Art Gallery, a grown-up dinner and cinema trip. It was the first whole day and evening out they'd taken since Liam was born and I wished I had thought of offering before, but better late than never.

On Sunday we set off for Bondi Beach, *en famille*, to spot many a bronzed Adonis. Alison strongly denied any awareness at all of these young men, after all she was a respectable married woman who only had eyes for Simon! It was an ideal day for walking, with a soft sea breeze, so we followed the path from Bondi to Bronte beach.

We witnessed two sea rescues on the way. It's the same worldwide, there will always be overconfident people who judge themselves competent when the safety flag is not flying, and when they get into difficulties, they get hauled out by bronzed *Baywatch* babes and fellas who risk their own safety. Why hadn't it occurred to me? It would have made my day to feature on the front page of the *Sydney Herald*, being carried from the sea in the arms of some gorgeous lifeguard. I could send the picture home to my daughters: *Look who I've pulled!*

After the high tension it was time to picnic on Bronte Beach, where the café food is top notch. Bondi Beach was much smaller than I imagined and absolutely jam-packed, with no one seeming concerned about sunstroke, skin cancer or how thin the ozone layer is. Everyone was playing ball, jumping in and out of the surf, swimming and generally having fun. Ah, the joy and carefree experience of youth; was I just the teeniest bit jealous? I went to bed pondering on the seemingly idyllic lifestyle of Sydney people and wondering if they had the right idea – that the rest of us take life too seriously.

Chapter 26

GROWING UP FAST

The day had arrived to say goodbye to Sydney and my adopted family. Alison drove me to catch my flight for Melbourne and as we hugged in a tearful farewell I was reminded of my own son and daughters back home.

It was so many years since I had seen my friends, John and Shirley, and I wondered if we would recognise each other. Was she feeling the same way? Butterflies were flitting around inside me from nervous excitement and I felt myself quiver.

We had met twenty years earlier when they last visited England. We had a wonderful teatime reunion at her sister, Ellie's, catching up on the old jaunts. That was when Shirley insisted that I spend time with them in Melbourne if I ever visited.

'That's a deal!' I had said, never imagining the day would come. But here it was.

On the two-hour flight, I found myself reliving days from our youth. Memories flooded back about how Shirley and I first became friends. When I came home to Croydon from my Dublin boarding school for the summer holidays our two families would meet on the road to church each Sunday. I was the oldest of six kids who my father escorted to the ten o'clock Mass at St Mary's. Shirley was one of twelve: seven girls and five boys. Our two fathers would chat on the way while we kids had fun together.

As teenagers, in the Sixties, I remember us all going dancing together. We never quit the floor from the moment we arrived at the dance hall until we left at the end of the night. The boys would stand, backs to the wall, on one side and the girls on the other side, and when the live band struck up, the boys would dash across the floor to pick their chosen girls to dance with. Jiving was the love of my life, and I took every opportunity I had.

I reminisced how I tried to pick out the best dancers and avoided chaps who stood on my feet, drank too much, had smelly armpits, or who tried to get fresh. If I saw a chap I did not fancy coming towards me, I made a beeline for the Ladies Powder Room. Luckily, I was never a wallflower and hardly ever stopped dancing. We often ended up running for the last train home, and I remember walking from the station in my bare feet as my stilettos were usually killing me by then. It was in carefree times with my girlfriends at these dance halls that many of us met our future husbands. How different my life was from my mother and father's generation.

I was shaken from reverie when the steward asked if he could get me a drink?

'Nothing, thank you. I have everything I need,' I said, and, gazing at the clouds, I drifted back to those teenage years.

How I wished Dad had seen me pass A Levels and go on to university. But he never did because, after my lovely father died, I became the breadwinner practically overnight. After all, the bills had to be paid and food put on the table for my mother, sisters and brothers. Being the oldest I was required to leave school and go to work. The decision was made for me at sixteen. My mother had never worked outside the house, plus she had her hands full looking after six of us.

What work could I usefully do at that age? I had no secretarial skills and did not want to work in a shop or a bar. The one subject I always enjoyed was maths, so, based on my projected exam results, I applied for a job in banking. Not any old bank for me though... my aspiration was to work in the Bank of England! I reckoned the experience would be more varied, and that the pay would be better than high street banks.

Within a week of applying, I was invited for an interview, and was totally overwhelmed and intimidated by the enormity of the institution. The butterflies that were fast becoming part of my life, launched into full flight that day. I decided to ditch my mini-skirt and wear something more conservative.

What an imposing building! *What have I let myself in for?* I worried. I was shown into a room and told to sit in front of three very serious-looking people, even more frightening than the building itself. I left their office sure I had made a mistake. *Why would people like this offer a young Irish girl a job? I really must be daft in the head*. A week later came the letter, formally addressed to me, and I steeled myself for the inevitable disappointment as I opened it. I was shocked into silence to read that I was being offered a job, subject to passing a medical and taking out British naturalisation. I was to sign the Official Secrets Act!

From that day and throughout my life, threads

have joined up and coincidences revealed themselves. One day an elegant and more senior colleague approached my desk.

'Would it be true that you're from Johnswell in Kilkenny?' she asked

'Well, yes... why do you ask?'

'Did you ever meet a man called Martin Brophy?'

'Of course, I did,' I retorted. I used to climb over his orchard wall to pinch fruit! And I was stung by wasps more than once... fighting them off for the plums from his trees!'

She told me that Martin was her brother and that she was one of two sisters, Maura and Eva, who were sent to school in England and grew up with their aunt in Ascot. It seemed she was an old friend of my mother.

'You'll never guess who I met at work today?' I teased Mum that evening. She was dumbfounded when I handed over Maura's phone number so they could meet again. Mum invited Maura and Eva to Sunday lunch and the three of them had a lively time.

This brought up memories of when I stayed with my grandmother in Kilkenny. There was a Capuchin friary, where a visiting friar was preparing to go on the Mission to Kenya. He was from Switzerland

and spoke Swiss German, (not very useful for communicating in Kenya!) so the abbot in charge asked my grandmother if she knew anyone who could help him improve his English.

'Oh, Brigid's got nothing to do all summer except swim in the weir and raid Martin Brophy's orchard!' she told the abbot, as she volunteered me and I watched my carefree holiday going down the river!

During our lessons he asked if I'd like a Swiss pen pal. I liked the idea of learning about other countries, even in those days; it would liven up my days at boarding school. He wrote to his brother in Zurich and a couple of weeks later I received an exciting envelope with Swiss stamps on it, from Gerolde. We corresponded over the next five years and got to know each other (I thought) quite well. When I was seventeen, she sent an invitation to spend two weeks with her family in Zurich. As I was working in the Bank of England, I managed to save enough money from my own wages for an airline ticket to Zurich, my first time out of the country.

Two boys stood staring at me as I emerged into the Zurich Arrivals' Hall. I noted them and walked past, hoping to spot Gerolde and maybe her parents.

'Excuse me, are you Brigid?' asked one of the young men.

'Yes, but why?'

'Welcome to Switzerland. I'm Gerolde,' he added.

I was dumbfounded and instantly fought to recall what I might have let slip in those chatty letters during our adolescence. All those years of writing to a girl – or so I thought! What a shock. I could only imagine what my mother would say when she found out I was on holiday with a seventeen-year-old boy!

We arrived at a detached mansion via a long drive that passed by their swimming pool, tennis court, croquet lawn and ornate landscaped garden. I rationalised that his parents must be the housekeeper and gardener and that I'd be staying with them in an adjacent service cottage. How wrong I was though. We walked through the front door of the large house and Gerolde took me straight to the drawing room to meet his mother.

It was a formal household – very different from my own. At dinner no one sat down to eat until Gerolde's father had said prayers. At the end of prayers, he rang a bell for the servants to serve our dinner. But it turned out that Gerolde's father was president of the Union Bank of Switzerland and, once we were talking, he was impressed that my first job was at the Bank of England. It gave me a touch of confidence for the stay.

Once the formality of dinner was over, the father took me aside.

'I have a special treat for you and Gerolde,' he confided. And he described a week-long train trip through the lakes and mountains of Switzerland with a hotel stopover each night. It felt extraordinarily grown up and I fretted about whether we were expected to share a room...

'Naturally, I've booked individual rooms for each of you,' he clarified.

Phew!

Everything on the journey was scheduled like a military exercise, and it was a breathtaking time of discovery: my first stepping stone to independence, away from Croydon, that would lead on to journeys around the globe.

Once home, Michael had become my steady boyfriend, but everything raced on rather faster than we had planned. He was offered a post with a British engineering company, as a contracts' manager... but in Canada. Company policy stipulated that I could accompany him, but only as his wife! We had no intention of getting married just then, but Michael was keen to take this unexpected promotion. It was a surprise career advancement and a definite step up the ladder.

And so, we were married in our local parish church of St Mary's, and I resigned my job at the Bank of England in preparation for our move.

My favourite uncle was a priest and he was given permission to marry us outside his own parish. I was sad my father was not alive to give me away, but Mum took his place. I would have preferred Denis, my oldest brother, but that's how it was.

Now we were all set for married life in Canada – or so we thought. Only then did my mother choose to drop her bombshell.

'But I do need you here, Brigid,' she told me. 'How will we manage? I can't be raising all your brothers and sisters on my own now, can I?'

Her timing was dreadful. I had given up a good job with prospects and was totally crestfallen. But, that's how we were brought up. In those days we were expected to do what our parents wanted or needed. Michael was understandably devasted. The new job would have offered a marvellous opportunity to further his ambition of managing and supervising electrical engineering contracts. We had to totally review our future. Did it impact on our future together? I often wonder how ambivalent he truly was in settling for second-best?

He never expressed the full range of his feelings. He turned down the contract and went back to his old job. It often crossed my mind whether that early disappointment played a role in him turning to alcohol. How much it changed our relationship or left room for resentment? Of course, I can only imagine. I will never have an answer to these sixty-four-million-dollar questions. I do know how responsible and sorry I felt for him having to decide whether to go to Canada alone, and still wonder how different our life might have been. But at the time it was no good crying. We just got on with it.

As for me, having already been dealing with stocks and shares and found it fascinating, I took a research position with a well-known stockbroking firm, and advising clients which companies to invest in. I loved the work so much that it became like a hobby, and I stayed there until our first child was born.

One day when our son Sean was young, I was visiting my mother. When her phone rang, she asked me to answer it.

'Aha! What a coincidence, Brigid. You're just the person I want to speak to.'

It was my old boss asking if I was free to go back and work for him. My replacement had apparently proved 'a disaster'. I was caught unawares and didn't know what to say.

'Before you turn me down... please come and have lunch with me. We can discuss options.' We met near his office and over our meal he proposed that I work whatever hours suited me. In case I needed more persuasion, he offered to pay for Sean's schooling at a prep school, and followed it up by dangling a generous salary. It would have been rude to refuse, but I agreed anyway because I knew how excited I'd be back in that stimulating environment. I would be paid well for work I loved doing.

Chapter 27

THE WELCOME STRANGER

'We will shortly be arriving in good time at Tullamarine airport, Melbourne. Please return to your seats and fasten your belts ready for landing. Thank you for flying with us today and we wish you a safe onward journey,' came from the cockpit.

The flight had been a pleasure and I was about to land in Melbourne, rested for my onward journey.

I had no problem picking Shirley out from the crowd in Arrivals and the beam on her face showed she recognised me too. Obviously, we were older, but it was still her and John. I ran up, gave her a big hug and it was as if twenty years just melted away. John and Shirley were the first of my friends to get married, and I had only seen them once since they emigrated to Australia, after which her sister Ellie became my best friend.

'We have a hell of a week planned for you,' she grinned

As we sat over drinks in their peaceful garden in a Melbourne suburb, we reminisced for hours about our childhoods, our children and our lives. Even though it was painful for me to relive the memories I told them the circumstances of Michael's death, and how I came to be here. We shared fond memories of him and hoped he was looking down on us, happy that we were spending time together.

Having felt him with us as we spoke, I was engulfed with sadness at bedtime, knowing the reality that Michael could not share this with us. It would have been in his plans to meet up with John and reminisce about their youth. John's brother, Vincent, lived near us in Surrey and Michael used to spend hours chatting to him about the Old Country. At breakfast, I still had mixed feelings.

Having caught up on our lives, Shirley introduced me to the city she had fallen in love with so many years ago. We wandered along the Yarra riverbank, and I couldn't help but admire the exceptional houses facing onto the waters. We strolled along Victorian laneways that run between the main streets, known for their street art, cafés and bars, and Shirley related their history from the 1850s' gold rush. I gasped in wonder at the elegance of the grand Block and Royal Arcades.

Melbourne impressed me as being more sedate and less hectic than Sydney, with noticeably fewer tourists. The pace of life was slower and encouraged me to relax. I knew I could grow to love a place like Melbourne and, if I struck out on my own, I wouldn't worry about not finding my way back to Shirley's.

I was pondering how to thank Shirley and John for their welcome, when I remembered that Shirley loved tennis. As luck would have it, the Australian Tennis Open was on during my stay, so it felt an obvious gesture to book tickets for us to watch some top-rate games together.

We sat in their garden that evening while I regaled them with what I'd seen and done. John had planned a day out at the gold rush town of Ballarat the next day; an ideal way to connect the civic buildings I had visited with the origin of the money used to build them.

We set off for Ballarat as a team: John as our chauffeur and a couple of backseat drivers thrown in.

'Want to show me how good you are at hiking?' he suggested at one stage of our journey.

'I don't like those kinds of jokes,' I said dryly, remembering my road trip with the other John.

'Who says I'm joking?' he retorted.

I was silent as a mouse for the rest of the journey. It was either that or walk in the scorching heat. No choice!

Gold mining came to Ballarat big time in the 1800s with over 6,000 diggers arriving week by week as the government offered rewards to anyone finding gold within 200 miles of what became dubbed 'Marvellous Melbourne'. We visited the Eureka Stockade Memorial, commemorating the Eureka Rebellion of 1854 in which gold miners rebelled against indirect taxation by colonial authorities who imposed impossibly high licence prices. After a period of civil disobedience, a violent siege by UK forces brought about the death of around thirty miners and many injuries. The miners may have lost the battle but they won the war: they achieved their democratic rights, and the siege went down in history as the birth of Australian democracy. We took a guided tour of Sovereign Hill, a reconstructed gold town where the people, costumes, streets, modes of transport and shops, including a working forge, a cobbler's shop and grocery store, emulated the nineteenth century.

The Gold Museum was impressive. Back in the Bank of England I had seen gold bars like those being made here: smooth, sleek and shiny. But I had never seen such huge chunks of gold in their raw state, and they were surprisingly ugly. We went down a disused mine and panned for gold as a novelty. I hoped, optimistically, to make enough to pay for the Australian part of my trip, but did not come up with a single nugget when I drained the water from my pan! Later I discovered that, back in 1869, Cornish diggers in Victoria discovered the largest gold nugget ever mined, at a massive 66kg. It was named The Welcome Stranger, which, I mused, fitted my role seamlessly.

I went to bed that night dreaming about all those chunks of bright shiny metal and what I could buy with them. Then I reminded myself of the old saying that 'money does not buy you happiness', because I was without my Michael.

'Hey, I have a great day planned for you, Brigid!' announced Shirley, at breakfast. 'We're taking you to the airport and putting you on a flight back to Sydney.' She couldn't hold it together for long when she saw my crestfallen face, and burst out laughing.

'Only pulling your leg,' she admitted. 'Why don't you take a wander round some of our public gardens, then, we'll meet you in the park for a picnic supper at the open-air jazz concert. What do you think?'

'Sounds fantastic,' I said.

An important item on my agenda was to buy tickets for the Australian Tennis Open. I thought it might be tough, but this was not Wimbledon; there was no queue, and I was astonished to be handed three tickets for Monday with no quibble.

How did I first hear about the tennis? It was on Christmas Day at Jean's, we were discussing the Australian Tennis Open where Jean and her keen tennis-playing friends spend a week every year, always in the same hotel near Melbourne Park. When she heard I was going to be in Melbourne at that time she suggested we meet up. I had promised to call if I was successful with getting tickets. Shirley and John were delighted at the plan, so Jean and I agreed to meet for coffee at the Rod Laver Arena on Monday.

But I'm getting ahead of myself. That Saturday evening was perfect for our concert in Fitzroy Gardens. We met up with Shirley and John's daughter, Julia, and her two girls, and had a special children's picnic on the grass before they went home to bed. We adults hunkered down on the lawns for the jazz concert held in the Sydney Myer Music Bowl. Myer had been inspired by visiting the Hollywood Bowl in California and took a risk that his design would work in Melbourne; luckily it turned out to be an enormous success.

It stayed balmy all evening. And the music was not bad either! The Bowl was packed and we were all up tempo as we ate our alfresco supper and downed a few tipples. The concert finished at 9.30 pm, when we packed up and made our way home full of music. It was a magical end to an active day, and reminded me of nights picnicking in evening dress and black-tie at Glyndebourne Opera House, in Sussex, though this was a considerably more laid-back type of fun.

Next morning John and Shirley took me to Mass at the oldest Catholic church in Victoria, which was their favourite. An Irish Franciscan priest had laid the foundation stone in 1841, and consecrated the church in the name of St Francis of Assisi, his order's founder. I took away vivid memories of its lively congregation of mostly Philippino families, and vibrant stained-glass windows shining onto a red carpet that flowed from the high altar down the centre aisle. After Mass we were joined by Julia and her girls for brunch in Fitzroy Gardens where a

Fairy Tree Concert was performed for the children, with the enthusiastic audience, including Julia's daughters, dressed up as fairies. Community shows and concerts are mounted regularly by Melbourne Council in the school holidays for families to get together.

One of the many bonuses of holidaying alone is being able to make decisions without conferring with other people. Travelling alone taught me the useful lesson that I needn't be afraid, lonely, depressed or panic stricken. As the weeks flew by, I saw how my life and way of living had changed since I left home in November and found myself to be a panic-stricken woman frozen to the spot in Hong Kong airport. The woman who wanted to make a U-turn onto the next plane home? What happened to her? She found her wings and learned to fly – in every sense. At times, she pinches herself to check that she really is surviving just fine.

Monday, so, it must be the Australian Tennis Open! We were off to the Melbourne Arena – yet another milestone for me. Shirley brought a top-class packed lunch – a skill she has down to a fine art.

After proper research and deliberation, we watched Venus Williams play against a little-known Bulgarian player, Svetlana Pironkova. It was a captivating game in which Venus suffered a shock defeat in the first round from the young Bulgarian who went on to trounce her. The crowd was stunned as they watched the points build up to the advantage of a new kid on the block.

Before the next match, I popped off to meet Jean, for our quick promised coffee.

'I gather you left John's house after Christmas and moved into Sydney?' she probed.

'Yes, that's right,' I said, and wanted to leave it at that, without going into the circumstances of why I'd moved out.

'Now you know why we're not together,' she said. We both understood what she meant, and that was the end of that particular topic. We had a short friendly get-together that cleared the air of uncertainty, I wished her a great week here in Melbourne, and went back to Shirley and John.

When the tennis restarted, we watched a long five-setter between James Blake from America and José Acasuso from Argentina. It was such a well-balanced match that it was a shame one of them had to lose! We finally left the arena at 7.30 p.m. to go home to a TV supper and, as if we had not seen enough tennis, we watched Serena Williams' nerve-racking win. I went to bed dead tired, as if I'd been playing tennis all day!

Chapter 28

ALISON SINGING

This silly goose, lacking a traveller's wisdom, had booked an early flight back to Sydney so had to be up at six next morning. What was I thinking of? I couldn't believe this fun-packed week was over.

'I'll be back.' I warned my friends. 'Don't move house or change your phone number... or I will know why!'

I wondered if I'd ever honestly be back. I hate goodbyes and it felt hard to leave these special people who looked after me so well. Shirley had confided her heart was in Australia and she would never return to the UK, even though I had a feeling that John might have loved to end his days in Ireland near his extended family. I will always remember us together as teenagers in the Irish dance halls of London. We had simply grown older.

I landed in Sydney to torrential rain, and ended up like the drowned rat who first walked into Grainne's travel agency. What a change from the gorgeous blue sky I had left. Here, I needed to exchange my sun hat for a raincoat and umbrella. Rain was flooding the streets, making them like rivers, but I didn't like to mention Wellington boots and upset Fred again.

'No worries, mate,' Fred told me (he too had picked up the language). 'This is just drizzle for a quality boot!'

He was right. He was coping admirably so far.

Ruby piped up at that point. 'To be blunt...' Uh-ho, what was coming? 'You really could do with new underwear. Those sure have seen better days.' That was a bolt out of the blue!

But she wasn't wrong. I was embarrassed every time I washed the same old threadbare knickers and made a mental note to visit a department store and treat myself.

I hoped that the sun was shining on London as it was my daughter Catherine's birthday. *Many Happy Returns, Catherine!* I thought. *Sorry to miss your celebrations. But short of chartering a private plane... I'm sure you understand?* I resolved to toast her good health this evening, and was looking forward with almost uncontrolled excitement to her joining me in New Zealand in a fortnight.

Alison picked me up, complete with umbrella, and Simon made us a delicious breakfast. He always seemed very much at home in the kitchen. He had already been to the bakery for *pains au chocolat*, as well as cooking up excellent Eggs Benedict and coffee.

We sheltered indoors and chatted over my trip to Melbourne. They had never been to that southern tip of Australia, which surprised me. What would I recommend? What was the highlight of my week? How did it compare to Sydney? They had so many questions and my answers whetted their appetite so much that they began to plan their own trip. For the next couple of days, the weather made my decisions for me – it was rain, rain and more rain – just like home. I used the time to catch up with some badly neglected correspondence. It was dry but still cloudy when Alison asked if I would like to visit the Japanese Gardens, which reminded her of where Simon and she first met. They were both at university in Kyoto; Simon doing a Masters in Law while Alison was reading Music. After a few years working in Japan, they married and set up house in Alison's homeland of Australia.

The Japanese Gardens were off the beaten track, not a regular find for a first-time tourist. I was enchanted by the art and technical skills demonstrated in the bonsai collection. I had never seen such meticulous symmetry, and could not imagine using tiny nail scissors to sculpt the shapes. When I picked my jaw up off the floor we had walked on and were surrounded by a seemingly endless variety of bamboos. I had thought bamboo was all the same but I now know better. It was enough to make me resolve to visit Japan someday.

Over lunch in Church Point the rain hit us again, in sheets, making us pick up our meals and run for cover. Back home we towelled ourselves dry and tuned in to more tennis from sunny Melbourne.

I asked Alison about her music degree. These days she taught piano and singing at home. I told her that I was a fan of my native Irish music and looked online for one of my favourite songs, the old traditional *The Rose of Tralee*. We listened to it being sung by Count John McCormack who was born and raised in Athlone, my mother's birthplace. In his day this famous Irish tenor was more popular than the Beatles, and his rendition brought warm memories of childhood trips when my father serenaded us as we drove to visit our Athlone family.

Alison loved the lyrics so much that I cheekily encouraged her to sing it for me, even though I knew she did not sing in public. She modestly offered to try, and sang so beautifully that she drew tears from my eyes. I realised afresh that you can take the person out of the country but you can't take the country out of the person. I could be anywhere in the world, but at heart I am always Irish.

The Sydney Festival was underway until Australia Day, and in the Botanical Gardens children were happily ensconced on the grass totally engrossed in a performance of *The Wind in the Willows*. I caught myself hoping that the moral of Kenneth Grahame's story would inspire them to try to always do their best as they grew up, to forgive others and make the world a better place. This charming sight brought a wave of sadness over me, thinking how my granddaughter would have loved it, and I had to move along before I made a fool of myself and cried. Never a good idea to frighten the children.

Siobhan had contacted Beth, told her the dates when I'd be in Sydney. So, I got a surprise phone call from Beth, who I'd heard so much about from when Siobhan stayed with her.

'I've been dying to meet Siobhan's mother...

Siobhan was like a daughter I never had.'

After Mass I made my way over to see Beth, who was extremely complimentary about Siobhan and said how much she'd missed her. Maybe my travelling the world was contrariwise in the genes, making me a chip off the *young* block! Like daughter – like mother.

While Siobhan was backpacking, and staying with John and Jean of my Christmas adventure, her travel fund ran low. She didn't have enough money to move on to New Zealand, so her only option was to find work. She was interviewed by an agency and offered a secretarial post in the medical school at Sydney University, where Beth was head of faculty.

Beth asked her to stay on after her four-week contract, and Siobhan was delighted as more savings would mean more fun in New Zealand. She was eventually offered a permanent position, running the faculty office, but although she loved Sydney, she knew she would be much too homesick to stay permanently. Nonetheless, Beth had plenty of room and invited Siobhan to stay at her place. It turned out to be a fantastic arrangement as she lived close to the university, in Marrickville, and travelled to work together in Beth's car, so she didn't even have travelling expenses. You can imagine how delighted

I was when Beth contacted me, knowing I could finally thank her in person for looking after Siobhan like a mother.

It turned out that she only lived ten minutes from Simon and Alison's. They dropped me off on their way to the park and I spent a relaxing afternoon with Beth, instantly understanding why Siobhan loved staying with her.

I never got to meet her husband Raymond, who had died two years earlier, but Beth showed me his vast collection of music. Siobhan had described him as a 'larger than life' personality who was principal violinist with the Sydney Orchestra and played for many years at Sydney Opera House. I'd like to have known him as we could have talked for ages about opera. Siobhan had already described their extraordinary house. In Australia they call them Federation Homes; built around the turn of the nineteenth to twentieth century and containing bags of character. Beth's single-storey home had high ornate ceilings, marble fireplaces, stained-glass doors and windows, and was expertly designed so that, with the doors and windows open, you get a cool breeze and did not need air-conditioning, even with temperatures of 30 degrees outside. As I walked in, I saw it was exactly as Siobhan had described. The area was full of these beautifully-maintained houses. Federation architecture is all listed, and still sought after as the years go by. This one was built in 1890 and solid as a rock.

We ate a late lunch under a tree in her secluded garden, and I felt as if I was in the countryside. In the afternoon we watched Andy Roddick being knocked out of the tennis and Roger Federer marching on. His cool, unruffled form convinced me he would smash the final.

We got on so well that Beth invited me to stay for a couple of nights the following week.

'Hey,' she said, 'you could even sleep in Siobhan's bed!'

We looked in at the bedroom that my daughter had used all those years ago and as she opened the door, I felt a lump rise in my throat. At last, I'm able to put a smiling face to the woman who sends me a scenic Australian calendar without fail every Christmas.

Chapter 29

SHARING MADAM BUTTERFLY

While I was far away, fantasizing in the Blue Mountains, Patricia (a neighbor from Brenda's birthday party) had rung to ask if I would like to meet up before she returned to Port Douglas? She, Tom and I had taken an instant liking to each other. We had such a good rapport that when they came to Sydney, we had a lovely lunch at Doyle's in Watson's Bay. Patricia left her phone number so I called her back and was looking forward to seeing her again.

I took a bus into town and joined another walk, which gave me the chance to reflect on how I was feeling at this point on my travels. Was I weary, or still enjoying life on the road? Should I consider changing anything? The answer came, clear and resounding: *No! So far, this trip has been beyond my wildest dreams and expectations.*

The overcast day was just perfect for walking, musing, and processing some of my many experiences, and I worked up a good appetite making our way to our meeting place in yet another new district of Sydney. We caught up at an Italian restaurant, where Patricia wanted to hear about my adventures since we had eaten the Morton Bay Bugs together – before Christmas.

'Aren't you nervous on your own?' she asked.

'You know what? I'm getting braver as each day goes by. I've stopped cowering at unfamiliar challenges.' And I told her the story of trying to scramble onto the next plane back home from Hong Kong.

'Do you think it's different at our age?' she probed, trying to get to the bottom of it.

'I reckon it's a case of building up lots of baby steps... taking one day at a time.'

'Well, frankly, I'd be completely out of my comfort zone...,' said Patricia.

How could I express what I wanted to say? 'I've worked out, that, for me, living with regrets would leave me unhappy... unfulfilled perhaps? I still have so many ambitions... and I'm growing in confidence all the time. I just have to trust I'll be safe and happy each day, I suppose...' I'm not sure that she was convinced.

I was beginning to realize that I could actually do this, and with the self-assurance to go forward I could even blaze a gentle trail to encourage other 'women of a certain age' to take the plunge and reap these benefits. All I held on to was a tiny seed of faith in myself, and life did the rest. Unexpectedly helpful people rose up to meet me on the road. I could feel the old Irish blessing at work:

"May the road rise up to meet you.
May the wind always be at your back.
May the sun shine warm upon your face,
and rains fall soft upon your fields.
And until we meet again, may God hold you
in the palm of His hand."

'You a philosopher now, then?' interrupted Fred.

'Don't be daft. That's St Patrick!'

'Well, I never,' he jeered. 'Aren't you the font of knowledge!'

Did I really blather with my rucksack and boots? Well, I did sometimes lay in bed at night and question my sanity. But they were my only travelling companions and had become like steadfast friends: Fred facilitated all my wayfaring and, Ruby carried my essential worldly goods. At times, of course, I sorely missed the safe security of my little home in Brighton. But an early return would only have left me with feelings of failure. Can you understand that? I had to take those first steps, even if they were fretful, and follow their lead on to the next.

I may not have convinced Patricia, but I vowed to her that I was committed to seeing this through to the end. Our conversation left me fully determined to make every planned stop along the way before I set foot in England to embrace my friends and family. If those friends were to ask my advice about taking a trip like this, I would, without hesitation, tell them not to give it a second thought. We only have one life, let's live it to the full. So says the petrified mouse who froze to the spot in Hong Kong!

'You go for it, girl. Remember, I'm with you all the way,' promised Ruby.

And Fred joined in. 'Oi, me too! *We're* with you.'

Our lunch had left me with new resolve.

`It was already Tuesday, when Beth had invited me to stay. She picked me up on her way home and we shared a homely supper in front of the tennis. I missed having Liam beside me, clapping with the crowd. And that night, I drifted comfortably off to sleep in 'Siobhan's bed'.

While Beth was at work I occupied my quiet time with postcards, and thank-you notes to the many people who looked out for me here in Australia. After stamping and dispatching them at the post office, it was still dreary outside, so I found a manicure and pedicure salon from where the competent Vietnamese technicians posted me back to Beth's in a very happy mood. Oh, yes, I had my eyebrows waxed too. I dared not meet Catherine next week with them looking awry or I'd hear her usual, 'Mum, you look like a sheep'. That's daughters for you – straight to the point!

I arrived, newly beautified, to Beth suggesting a walk back to the shops for supper items. Beside the convenience store was a café which we couldn't pass without a coffee and their scrumptious homemade lemon tart – just to keep us going until dinner time, you know.

I'd been admiring her eclectic collection of classical music albums and found a recording of Count John McCormack singing *When Irish Eyes are Smiling*.

'Not mine,' she said. 'They were Raymond's. I just don't have the heart to get rid of them.'

Music had been his passion. We spent a companionable time after dinner listening to some of his favourite recordings, after which the idea of tennis felt rather mundane.

It was the eve of Australia Day, a public holiday on which Beth did not have to work. Akin to Queen Elizabeth's birthday honours, people receive awards for services to the country. Others are made Australian citizens, and this year 14,000 people were to be granted this privilege.

Marking the day in a fitting way, Beth showed me around Botany Bay National Park, known as *Kamay* by the Aboriginals who first settled there around 5,000 years ago, and renamed Sting Ray Harbour after Cook's landing in 1770. Soon afterwards the European explorers discovered thousands of new plant varieties, earning it the botanical name which has stuck.

Some university students renting the house next door invited us to join their barbecue when we got back. They too treated Beth as an adopted mother, as Siobhan had done: a great listener, agony aunt, confidante, adviser, nurse, doctor – all rolled into one kind, caring person who happened to live next door. It worked both ways, because they replaced the children she never had, as well as the huge gap left by Raymond's death. The boys made a great supper and waited on us hand and foot. It was obvious that they all loved Beth. We sat in the garden until sunset before going home to – yes, it was still going on – more tennis.

Beth went off to bed early, ready for work, while I watched Henin-Hardenne beat Sharapova. Kim Klisters had to retire injured and Meuresmo claimed the match. So, the final was between Henin-Hardenne and Meuresmo. I didn't really care who won, but was enjoying the laid-back atmosphere of this tournament much more than I'd expected. What a difference to the formal and strait-laced tennis back home.

Over my brief coffee with Jean at Melbourne, she invited me to spend a day with her before I left for New Zealand, and I was looking forward to chatting to her one-to-one. At last we could talk about the things that really mattered to us both. She apologised for John's behaviour at Christmas, but I insisted that she was in no way responsible for him. She wished she had told me sooner why they had split up, but hadn't expected him to behave badly towards me, what with Siobhan having been practically family all those years ago.

When Siobhan's friend Heidi was homesick and went home, Siobhan was still staying with Jean and John. She worked on his admin, typing up quotes and invoices, and running his home office until she got the job under Beth at the university.

'I bet he got Dutch courage from his mates,' reckoned Jean. 'They'd have egged him on with comments about you.'

She wasn't wrong.

'Maybe he thought he was in with a chance... you know, trying it on with you. Backfired on him though, didn't it!'

It was good to clear the air, at least with Jean, and I always remember her affectionately. Feeling more at ease with each other, we drove to Kernell, the spot where Cook first landed in HMS *Endeavour*. He rested anchor for eight days before sailing into Sydney Harbour, where a museum informed me about Cook's life as my fellow, if not contemporaneous, adventurer. We met a friend who had spent Christmas evening with Siobhan all those years ago, and who was interested to meet me at last; she said Siobhan was an exact younger version of me.

So, I was in fine spirits when I left them and set off on my grand treat to see *L'elisir d'Amore* at the Sydney Opera House, with the ticket I'd bought before Christmas. Building works began for Sydney Opera House in 1959 but it wasn't opened by Queen Elizabeth until October 1973, with a production of

War and Peace. Paul Robeson was among the first to perform there, and Arnold Schwarzenegger won his last Mr. Olympia body-building title there back in 1980.

Jean had never attended an opera, so I suggested she join me the following evening for *Madame Butterfly* in the park. It was staged as a modern production, which disappointed me as it was Jean's first introduction. I am not a fan of modern staging, but that's being a purist – or simply picky. I was hoping to see it set around 1904, when Puccini composed it and premiered it at La Scala, Milan.

Donizetti's music rang in my head as I sat on the bus to North Bridge next morning to see a teaching friend from the 1970s, at her mother's house. Back then I taught secretarial skills, bookkeeping and financial accounts in the same department as Stephanie, aka 'Steve', whose chum Marion had a flat in Pimlico. Yes, it was Marion I was on my way to meet and who was spending the winter months in Sydney with her mother. Unknown to me, she had been following my travel blog which inspired her to link up with me.

She had duly noted from my scribblings my penchant for Sydney rock oysters and king prawns and, accordingly, spoiled me rotten by serving up oysters to start, king prawns and salad, mango *and* pineapple and plenty of wine. Not for the first time, I found myself questioning how I would ever be satisfied with 'normal' when I got home!

As if this wasn't enough, Marion took me to her favourite beach, Balmoral, named for the royal palace in Scotland. This, she confided, is where she dreamed of buying a property if she won the lottery. That's the level of money it would take, so we made do with a gorgeous walk and sitting happily on the beach, looking out over the bay, as we swapped stories of our lives since those college days.

We got on so well that I suggested she come to *Madame Butterfly* in the Domain that evening. She was thrilled and, luckily, her neighbour offered to stay with her mother for the evening. We made up a picnic basket, and picked up drinks from a wine shop on the way to our 'Opera in the Park'.

I hoped Jean and Marion would find their first opera as enjoyable as I would. Thoughtlessly, I had not asked either of them about their musical preferences, so it seemed quite a responsibility. *Oh well*, I resigned myself. *It'll either be a total disaster or they'll come away walking on air and thank me profusely!*

The park was heaving with around 85,000

people. No, I have not added too many noughts! Every January, thousands of Sydneysiders flock here for this night of free opera; they heave in their deckchairs, picnics and drinks, then sit back and enjoy the entertainment on a massive screen. The atmosphere felt something like *The Last Night of the Proms* in Hyde Park, London. I noticed that it was a youngish crowd, mostly around 25 to 45 years old, plus a few oldies like us, but no drunks or hooligans, and no litter left scattered about: everyone took their rubbish home or stashed it in the large recycling bins.

I began to understand that this was part of an annual festival, much like our Brighton Festival each May, and tonight was one of many free concerts including the Sydney Symphony Orchestra, a George Gershwin evening, a jazz evening and, this year, *Madame Butterfly*. On this gentle evening we were part of a truly attentive and eclectic audience of thousands, many unceremoniously on rugs on the grass. We found a perfect viewing place, not far from the screen. What could be lovelier? It was elating to be part of this intoxication – the appreciation was tangible – so lucky to be in Sydney that night and part of this dazzling evening.

It was apparently sponsored by the Mazda Motor

Corporation, and during the interval there was a grand draw in which one woman won a Mazda MX5 car; the lucky b....! Imagine attending a free opera *and* leaving with a shiny new sports car? Not bad, eh? I took time out to wonder how I'd have got the car home if I had won it... but since I did not there was no need to worry about it for too long!

As we sauntered happily away, I asked my friends, in some trepidation, how they'd found the evening. They burst out enthusiastically that I had made two new opera fanatics, and they would treasure special memories of this night. We were in a jaunty cheerful mood, so I think it's safe to say that our little group enjoyed the whole glorious balmy evening. For me, it meant even more. I recognised that I could easily get used to this Sydney lifestyle.

Chapter 30

ON THE TRAIN WITH MR BEAN

As my little Australian family were now in the Snowy Mountains staying with friends from Japan, it felt strange and lonely having the house to myself and I missed Liam's chatter. But before long I had a call from Kerrie.

'It's a glorious day up here in Leura, Brigid. Why not hop on a train and see the place at its best?' I did not need persuading!

I got my act together in a trice and was at the station straight after church, only to find the train drivers were on strike! But plans should always be flexible, so I took the coach halfway and transferred to a local train for Katoomba, where I chatted happily to a Taiwanese family on holiday for Chinese New Year. I made my way to my favourite spot at Echo Point, and promised Fred this was the final hike before New Zealand.

It was my last chance to feast on the sight of its massive sandstone valleys and the Three Sisters rock formations, shaped by wind, weather and volcanic eruptions since the Triassic period, 200 million years ago. This bright clear day revealed them in all their jaw-dropping glory.

I was so happy to see Kerrie and Jennie again before I left Australia. I felt very much at ease with them and I really hoped that one day I could return their lovely welcome by inviting them to Sussex. Geoff popped in to say hello while we were eating and that evening I recorded in my diary: 'I do like that man – he is such great fun. Kerrie, let me know if you make him redundant!'

I couldn't believe how much I could cram into a single day, because at five-thirty I was back on the train to Sydney. And that's when the fun started.

Most seats had been reserved but a few were empty, and a woman with her middle-aged son played their own version of musical chairs; just for fun, I counted them changing seats… five times.

Fred took a dislike to them. He was tired and edgy.

'Are those guys ever going to sort themselves out? I hope they don't end up over here!'

The mother was aggravating her son by insisting on taking *his* allocated seat, and nothing would budge her, not even his hilarious pleas. There's always one (or in this case, two) and I always seem to find them. Or do they find me? Well, we had drawn the short straw here. His final fidgety resting place was, naturally, next to us.

'Doesn't he remind you of Mr. Bean?' I whispered to Fred, pretending to do up my bootlaces.

'Could be his double,' he agreed, in a leathery stage whisper.

Watching the goings on became our evening's entertainment.

Having sat down with his dinner on a tray, our man decided that the food was cold so traipsed back to the dining room to resolve the problem. Then he found himself lacking salt and pepper. Once more he clambered over me from the window seat. Within seconds of climbing in again, his mother said they were getting off at the next stop so there was no time to eat. Before disembarking he made me a gift of his half-eaten tray.

'Lost your appetite, have you?' enquired Fred.

Meanwhile, my attention turned to the fellow in front of me who was uninhibitedly wailing Japanese songs to the tune of his Apple Nano. He was in the zone and oblivious to other people.

'It's crazy on this train... and I can feel a splitting

headache creeping on,' said Fred.

I told him we'd be home and quiet soon, but that such is the rich pattern of a life on the tracks. I felt I was part of a TV comedy and wasn't sure which would best reflect reality.

'Good journey?' enquired Alison, as we rolled in.

'Don't ask!' I said, heading straight to the kettle for a soothing cuppa.

The stark realisation hit me that this was my very last day in Australia. Gremlins were invading my head space and I tuned in to a rising panic about moving into unfamiliar territory again (both actual and emotional). I was linking up with my daughter Catherine, and would not be alone driving around New Zealand, so why the frenzy?

Alison tuned in to my acting like a headless chicken; phone calls, laundry, packing, thank-you notes, checking my papers. She extricated me from my whirlwind by practically dragging me to the Italian deli around the corner. Maybe she too needed a calmer environment. A hearty dessert put us both straight, by which time I needed another shower as it was a sopping 35 degrees.

Later, we met Simon for a farewell dinner before carrying a heavy-eyed Liam home to his bed. I wondered if he would ever remember the Irish 'auntie' who came across the globe to visit him. By now they felt like my extended family, and had certainly treated me as one of theirs. My time in Sydney was personal and richer for being with them. I felt as if I had been here for years and departure felt abrupt, though inevitable. Emotions were jockeying for position in my brain and I already felt a painful nostalgia for everything I would miss. I had to acknowledge that I might never visit again, nor see the people I had met who were so significant in making my grief less painful.

The highlights were too abundant to list, pivoting around my birthday with Brenda at the Great Barrier Reef, and the thoughtful friendly people who reached out to me as a stranger. I felt affection for them all, and gratitude wafted in deep waves through my heart for their warm welcome and kindnesses in a faraway country.

'Goodbye, my adopted mother,' said Alison, as we hugged tightly. I was soaked in the words, and they have stuck in my mind.

Chapter 31

A NEW ZEALAND REUNION

Now that I had walked the territory spread beneath me from the plane window, the view over Botany Bay blew me away by its location.

One overwhelming light inspired the flight to New Zealand: I was so excited to be meeting Catherine and to drive around the two islands together. A new step out of my comfort zone became instantly simpler. So far, I had avoided even moderate disasters on my trip, which later gave me the courage to make subsequent trips to many countries and meet people of all nationalities. I didn't anticipate any insurmountable challenges with Catherine on the team.

Months ago, as soon as she heard the words 'New Zealand', Catherine's ears pricked up.

'Oh Mum, I could do that trip with you!'

'Hmm, not sure. I'll think about it...' I answered, nonchalantly.

Her face fell.

'I'm joking! That would be absolutely amazing...' I was over the moon.

Back then she had no ties; no husband, boyfriend, or pressing commitment to get in the way. Catherine was a free spirit. We immediately started plotting how she could wangle a whole month off work.

'Just tell your boss the truth... that your mother is touring New Zealand and needs a backup driver... that I'm not happy to drive alone,' I said. 'If he agrees, then you can start saving and pack a rucksack.'

He agreed – and she did.

Just imagine a mother and daughter backpacking together... sometimes she can be a pain in the backside, and I'm sure she thinks the same of me, but she has fantastic qualities and is full of fun. It certainly wouldn't be dull or boring. Thelma and Louise could eat their hearts out! We were on our way.

New Zealand has become a global standout in its success at fighting the Coronavirus, partly due to stringent border restrictions applied to almost all foreign travellers since March 2020. It helped that the country is surrounded by water. Jacinta Arden closed their borders early and implemented the world's strictest lockdown, so curtailing the spread of the virus. It seems an inspiring example of a nation working harmoniously to achieve a common goal. Back then, no one could have contemplated such a force of nature as the Covid-19 pandemic.

Auckland, in the north, is the main airport, but I was landing at Christchurch, on the South Island. I was fast becoming a seasoned traveller with such facts at my fingertips. I was the first to arrive.

As she got off the plane Catherine looked like a zombie who had been partying all night! I had to remind myself that she had taken a twenty-four-hour flight from London, and another ninety minutes after changing at Auckland. I had organized the car and booked a nearby hotel. Once on the road, we were planning on bed & breakfasts. My long-awaited daughter literally fell on her bed and crashed out.

I closed the curtains, pulled a cover over her, then crept quietly out for a reconnaissance of Christchurch. I wandered the beautiful parks and tree-lined streets that earn it the tag 'Garden City', and learned how it was named after Christchurch College, Oxford.

In the park, I reminisced about Jason, the first New Zealander I met, who turned up looking for work at Siobhan's London recruitment agency. She found him a temporary job with Shell where they later offered him a permanent post, but he did not want to put down roots in England. Dale, his girlfriend from back home, worked as a beauty consultant in Selfridges and they were both saving hard to get married and raise a family in their homeland. Eventually, they did. But before leaving they said Siobhan or her family would always be welcome to visit them in Auckland. So, once our dates were firmed up, I contacted Jason who, true to his word, was delighted for us to stay with them and meet the family.

When Catherine woke up it was evening. She was dazed and disorientated.

'I was so shattered I couldn't think straight, Mum. I can't believe I'm here ... in New Zealand ... it's like I'm dreaming,' she said. 'Except the dream has come true! I've wanted to come for so long... and here I am with you. It's surreal.'

Straightaway, we made a pact that we'd never go to bed in a huff. We sealed it with a couple of glasses of champagne. I had high hopes that we would still be speaking to each other by the end of the road trip. Low mumbling followed by high-pitched girlish giggles started coming from behind the curtains and we drew them back to see that Ruby was having a great craic with Catherine's rucksack.

'What does she call you?' asked Ruby.

'Nothing really,' replied the new girl on the block.

'Well, I'm gonna call you Rita. We're sort of cousins now!' said Ruby.

So, Rita it was.

'When I want to complain about you, Brigid, I'll tell my new cousin.'

'Brigid,' said Fred, 'I *never* complain about you.'

'Yeah? Well, you're just a crawler...' started Ruby, at which point I broke it up as we needed nourishment to soak up the champagne.

We sauntered to one of the pretty restaurants along the Avon River and our over-riding impression was the mass of trees and green spaces. Catherine was wilting fast by the time she'd eaten, so she headed back to the hotel, and while she slept, I did some provisional planning, including a visit to the nearby tourist office. The woman there recommended staying in backpacker hostels or B&B's. Our real interest was interacting with New Zealanders, who we hoped would be open to suggesting where to eat, shop, where to go and what to see.

Re-energized, we started off on our real adventures next morning - first stop, the Franz Josef Glacier via

Greymouth.

As we were nearing Arthur Pass, the drive became more stimulating in more ways than one. No, I don't mean the stunning geography, but the red light on the petrol gauge started blinking at me! I broke out in a cold sweat. How to explain to Catherine that we are about to be stranded in the middle of what felt like nowhere, without fuel? There was not a house, shop or person in sight. I held my breath, did not freak out, but gently nursed the car along for what seemed a hundred miles until, minutes before the engine died, civilization popped up in the shape of a petrol station.

'Why have we stopped?' asked Catherine, as she woke from a rhythm-induced doze.

'Just filling up with petrol... making sure we don't run out,' I answered casually.

Ruby and Rita wittered on from the back seat about irresponsibility, recklessness, negligence ...... I didn't know Ruby had such a good vocabulary. We made a secret vow not to say a word but to be more mindful in future. The lesson was noted: plan ahead for all eventualities.

With a full tank and happy heart, we drove to the Franz Josef Glacier and walked to its base. The amazing steel-blue and white river of solid ice flowed down the mountainous valley, taking our breath away with its colour. Maoris call it *Ka Roimata o Hine Hukatere*, the tears of Hine Hukatere, who was a fearless mountain climber of legend. She persuaded her lover Wawe to join her high in the mountains but they were struck by an avalanche and he was swept to his death. New Zealand is a country steeped in stories.

Closer to the base, we could taste the crisp pure air and were awestruck by the glacier's enormity.

'Are we climbing right up to that peak?' asked Fred.

'No Fred. Since when did you have crampons? They'd be most uncomfortable and I wouldn't do that to you.' I explained.

We were seeing only a small part of the glacier but noticed that planes were flying over its whole expanse, landing on a snow plateau atop the mountain, and people were getting out to visit it up close. I couldn't help imagining what the glacier would be like in its full majesty. It is protected from visitors these days, because giving access has taken its toll, and the top is only accessible as a snow landing by helicopter. With global warming glaciers are receding at an alarming rate. It was already happening fifteen years ago, and long before that, I guess, but now the ice is thawing, they may eventually disappear.

Our first B&B was at an original wooden homestead in Omarama, south of Fox Glacier and Lake Tekapo. It was a working sheep and cattle station, and had room for us too. We were greeted by an abundance of roses in the front garden, which I instantly interpreted as a good omen. Our second welcome was from Tony, the owner, who checked that we were happy to share a bedroom.

'Of course. We're mother and daughter, so we won't fight!' we replied, optimistically.

Kitchen, dining room, veranda and living room were shared with the other travellers, tea and coffee were provided, and we could cook our own food in the well-equipped kitchen.

Guess what! That was when we clocked that this pair of dilly dreamers had forgotten to buy food for supper!

I overheard Ruby tell Rita, 'We've got a right couple of plonkers here!'

Luckily, Tony came to the rescue by selling us some fresh eggs from his hens. We could rustle up a couple of omelettes and, as he felt sorry for us, he threw in some fresh rolls. That was a result! We made mental notes to check if we needed to buy food for our evening meal next time, especially if we were miles away from a café or supermarket.

At least we did not go to bed hungry, but we were dead tired and fell asleep in a flash, sleeping soundly until the working dog acted as our early morning alarm. We'd had a quiet night's rest broken by the occasional restful munch of grazing sheep.

After helping ourselves to toast and a few restorative cups of freshly-brewed coffee, we set off for Queenstown. Today, Catherine was happy to be the driver – at least she would not run out of petrol.

By now I was on top of the world, revelling in Catherine's company and daring to hope that our New Zealand odyssey might even be part of the healing process for her too, following her father's death. Like me, she was still missing him. We both enjoy an outdoor wilderness; the hiking, exploring; and particularly, having a good laugh.

Queenstown overlooks Lake Wakatipu, and is very popular with young travellers. It is surrounded by mountains and well-known for its skiing. It reminded me of my trip across Switzerland with my girl/boyfriend, Gerolde. The next day we took a boat trip to *Piopiotahi*, or Milford Sound fiord, and arrived to rare bright sunshine, unexpected as it is renowned for having the highest rainfall in New Zealand.

Rudyard Kipling described Milford Sound as the 'eighth wonder of the world', and I can certainly understand why. It is home to what must be the most impressive waterfalls on earth. Catherine and I were mesmerized and totally lost for adjectives to describe what we were seeing.

Our boat cruised far out to the Tasman Sea, where dolphins were keeping warm in the lake waters, adult and baby seals were sunbathing, and a vibrant rainbow offered up its promise. Seeing is believing!

'Imagine how proud Dad would be to see us out here together, Mum,' said Catherine.

'We're never going to forget sharing this,' I told her.

We planned a well-earned nap when we arrived back, but when our hosts unexpectedly invited us for dinner... well, how could we refuse? Fred asked me to wear slippers and give him some time out, so I begged a window to change my hiking boots and freshen up. We soon forgot about resting, warmed to their enthusiasm, and told our most engaging stories of the day.

'If you enjoyed Milford, why not try a trip out to Doubtful Sound from Manapouri tomorrow? Then you can compare the two,' they suggested.

'Haha! We're one step ahead of you!' I laughed. 'It's already planned, and our overnight stop is at Smuggler's Rest.'

'You're gonna love it there' approved our host.

Tentatively he asked, "How come you have an Irish accent but Catherine has an English one?'

'Oh, her? She's adopted!' I bluffed.

'You didn't really just say that, did you?' exclaimed Ruby, from under the table.

Catherine nearly choked on her food, before quickly putting him straight.

'Actually, I'm chaperoning her!' she teased.

'I couldn't let my mother loose in New Zealand on her own...'. 'She'd end up incarcerated for disturbing the peace! Definitely not to be trusted.'

'Ruby, did you hear that?' I needed support, even if it was from a piece of hand luggage.

But I wasn't going to get it, 'Yes – Catherine's quite right,' she said.

Did I expect gratitude? Maybe. But I countered with, 'I'm never going to invite her travelling again!'

I can still picture their bewilderment when we left the table. Unforgettable!

In the breakfast room next morning I imagined some strange looks from fellow guests.

'Catherine is my hair a mess?'

'No... I just think they've been warned about us!'

I couldn't imagine why.

'Mum,' said Catherine, 'not everyone understands

your sense of humour so, could you button it and behave yourself... please?'

'It was a bit late for that, but we had a good laugh anyway.

To our surprise our cheerful new hostess at Smuggler's Rest handed us a pack of goodies for breakfast and lunch. We were pleasantly astonished by this gesture, but she assured us she regularly made up food packs for her guests and hoped that we would enjoy them on our cruise. She advised us to wear windproof jackets, even though there was a clear blue sky with only the odd fluffy cloud, and went the extra mile by dropping us at Pearl Harbour (this Pearl Harbour serves Lake Manapouri).

'Ruby, my windproof jacket please!'

We boarded a large boat for Doubtful Sound and wandered the deck, drifting past small islands and ogling the towering mountains. The crew pointed out penguins, seals and even a shoal of dolphins following in our wake. This thrilling floor show made us reluctant to leave deck in case we missed the next act! So, we ate our sandwiches standing on the ship's deck, repeating ourselves like needles stuck on a turntable: *awesome, stunning, unbelievable, mind blowing, beautiful, out of this world!* I lost count and had to let the photos of mountains and sky in the mirror-like water do the talking.

Chapter 32

AT THE TOP TABLE

We didn't get to investigate Queenstown because of our leisurely journey there and our trip to the fiord. Time sped by, and suddenly we needed to consult the book about our next port of call and make the necessary bookings in advance. We did everything together so there would be no blaming each other for making the wrong choice!

We left for Manapouri town, on a lake of the same name. The boat for Doubtful Sound had been booked and the weather was seasonally fine. Early, before the ship, we dropped off Ruby and Rita at our hidden gem of a B&B, Possum Lodge, which we loved the second we arrived.

Possum Lodge was more like a holiday park than a hostel. Our spotlessly clean unit had twin beds and a shower, while the kitchen, dining and lounge areas were in a communal building. It looked peacefully down over the lake. To our surprise, our new hostess handed us a pack of goodies for breakfast and lunch. We were flabbergasted by this gesture, but she assured us she regularly made up food packs for her guests and hoped that we would enjoy them. It was such a considerate touch. She even went a step further and dropped us at Pearl Harbour – no, not the one in Honolulu; this Pearl Harbour serves Lake Manapouri - and she advised us to wear windproof jackets, even though there was a clear sky with only the odd fluffy cloud.

I lost count of the adjectives we used to describe Doubtful Sound. The photos can do the talking.

Chapter 33

LIKE THE ROAD TO KILLARNEY

We slept like babies that night, and asked our hostess to call ahead next morning to inform our lodge in Owaka that we were on schedule that afternoon. It was an opportunity to thank her for looking after us so well in Manapouri and, most importantly, to assure her that our lunch was better than anyone else's on the boat! Our next priority was to ensure a full tank of petrol because there were very few garages before Owaka.

'At least I've learned from my mistakes,' I admitted, without thinking.

Catherine pricked up her ears. 'What mistakes are those, Mum?'

'Oh, I forgot to mention that we nearly ran out of petrol on the first day.'

'Typical!' said Ruby to Rita.

We were both struck by the route being very like

the Killarney Road, in south-west Ireland. It reminded us of attending the yearly AA Convention there, with people from all over the world including our friends Patrick and Philomena – the ones who lived over the off-licence. They had a house in Donegal too.

'Mum, d'you remember one year when Dad, you and I were all at the top table on the last day of the Irish convention? I was about fourteen,' Catherine reminded me. 'Dad spoke for the AA, you for Al-Anon, and I was the Alateen speaker.'

National Conventions are still held every year in Ireland, and internationally. Patrick, Philomena, Michael and I were also at the 1995 International AA Convention in San Diego, California. But I remembered this one vividly because it was so unusual for one family to all be together at the top table, sharing how their lives had changed since joining their respective groups and learning about alcoholism. We each understood the problem from a different angle, and each represented a key part of the fellowship.

'I'll *always* remember that meeting, Catherine,' I told her.

'I was so proud of you and Dad,' I became overwhelmed by those memories, and realised that it was taking this drive through New Zealand, so many years later, to understand what they meant to us all.

There was silence in the car while we reflected on friends, we had lost from our AA family.

Catherine broke our contemplations and pulled us back to the present.

'That's enough of the past, Mum - now let's look to the future. What luxury five-star place have you booked for us tonight?'

We were heading for a beach lodge in Surat Bay, Owaka, and kept on track until we reached Gore, famous for its fly fishing, brown trout in particular. Here we allowed ourselves lunch at a little place that served trout straight out of the river. You can't get fresher than that! I remembered, as a child in Ireland, my father went to the market fish stall in our nearest town every Friday. We lived about eight miles from town, but he always brought home fish caught in the local river for supper. Our lunch trout was perfect. The waitress told us how people visit Gore purely to learn the art of fly fishing.

It caught our attention that Gore also boasted a Scottish Whisky Museum, one where you could sample the goods. The museum staff explained how whisky distilleries had arrived with the early settlers from Scotland, in 1848, but as we still had a long journey we forewent the opportunity to sample the Scotch.

Catherine used our driving time to educate me with her taste in music so that by the end of our month I knew every song by Foo Fighters, Coldplay, Kelly Clarkson, Pink, The Killers, Kings of Leon, The Fray and Maroon 5, and as the music grew on me, I started humming along. I felt quite trendy, and reckoned that not many of my peers would know these bands, let alone sing their tracks at the drop of a hatpin. I was quite enjoying myself, until Ruby piped up "Catherine. Have you noticed how my canvas ear-flaps are starting to sag with your mother making all that row?'

So for the second time in a week, Catherine politely asked me to 'button it' before we had a rebellion on our hands. Cheeky! There I was, my voice improving with every bar that I belted out ... it was harsh to shatter my ego like that and side with a rucksack, but my sensitivities recovered pretty meekly as we arrived at the lodge.

Our last hostess had booked it for us, and definitely got it right. We were bang on Surat Bay beach, in an extensive garden overlooking the sea. The owner told us we were the first mother and daughter team to stay with them, and the first Europeans too. We felt extraordinary; modern-day adventurers exploring the New World. Straightaway she booked our next stop at a place called 'Swaggers' in Oamaru, home to a blue penguin colony, so gifting us peace of mind and extra time to enjoy the hinterland here.

'But, you're in Owaka now, and you can expect a once-in-a-lifetime treat of nature tonight' she promised. 'Make your way down to the beach after supper. I think you'll be surprised.' And she left this tantalising promise hanging.

'Me too?' asked Fred.

'Yes, I'll need you...but no squeaking, thank you, or you'll scare the wildlife away.'

After a shower we walked into the town centre to a fish restaurant she recommended. The fish remained superb because sea and river fishing were serious hobbies round here, and we found our favourites, trout and salmon, being served that evening. After yesterday, I showed off a tad and enquired whether the trout came from the river Mataura in Gore; the waitress looked impressed.

'No-one's ever asked where the trout's sourced from!' she said. And we explained how we'd stopped to watch fly-fishers in the Mataura. We had fantastic service for the rest of our meal, including a generous glass of local wine on the house!

'That should complement your trout nicely,' said the waitress, with a smile.

Is a little knowledge truly a dangerous thing? Well this time: we benefitted from our smattering of knowledge! Friendliness and banter can take you a long way, and maybe, if you are the cynical type, you could say the old Irish charm helps too.

The meal was over but the day was not; judging by our hostess's hints, the best was still to come! At dusk, we wandered down to the beach as instructed and followed signs to 'The Hide' where a few seasoned bird-watchers were already in place, sporting professional cameras with costly telephoto lenses.

Conversations between them leaked that we were likely to spot yellow-eyed penguins emerge from the sea and make for their overnight scrubland resting places. We gathered that they are shy; too timid to show themselves if there are humans in sight or making a noise. We felt spellbound being present tonight, at this seasonal natural event and waited patiently before bearing witness to them wading out of the waves and waddling up the beach to their nests in the dunes.

With incredulity we watched these yellow-eyed

penguins, also known locally as *hoiho* or *tarakaka*, come ashore and were equally inspired at the stumps straddling the shoreline which we found to be traces of petrified forest. I had never heard of this phenomenon, but soon learned that a forest becomes petrified when ancient woodland becomes buried in water-saturated sediment or volcanic ash so that oxygen no longer causes it to decay. The result, as we saw, is fossilised tree stumps that can be hundreds of millions of years old. Our minds danced with surreal images of penguins and forest remains as we walked back to the lodge. Fred was befuddled, trying to understand the science, but we agreed that nature is a truly marvellous teacher.

We relived our magical time over breakfast before waving a reluctant goodbye and hitting the Dunedin Road to Oamaru. Dunedin is sometimes called the Edinburgh of New Zealand and we spotted plenty of buildings with Scottish names from when the town was first settled by the Scots.

At Swaggers the only available room had a double bed. The last time Catherine and I shared a bed was when six years old, and I mused that it would be lovely to sleep next to her again.

'I hope she doesn't snore!' blurted out Ruby.

'Actually, I think she probably does.'

Huh. I wonder if there's a cupboard for us?' Ruby moaned to Rita.

After a sleepless night (due to my daughter snoring) it was a relief to get up for breakfast. Ruby was still complaining. 'I need a lie-in... I did *not* get a good night's sleep!'

But breakfast was ready on the terrace, served by a jolly woman who again apologized about the bed. We told her it was our call and we should have booked earlier.

She showed us a short uphill walk from the town centre to see an overview before visiting the Victorian Precinct.

We took advantage of the low morning tide and found the natural geological wonder that are the Moeraki Boulders: they were like huge, round rock eggs laid on the sandy beach by a prehistoric creature. A local resident told us where best to see the blue penguins once dusk fell. We imagined ourselves old hands, as we'd already seen the yellow-eyed penguins and now knew the ropes. As evening encroached, we waited silently and patiently and were treated to the sight of dozens of little blue penguins waddling ashore to their nests.

We had another reason for visiting Oamaru. Years ago, when Siobhan was twenty-two, she lived here for three months, paying her way with a temporary job in a book store that earned her enough money to travel onwards. It felt a lighthearted reminder of how our family travel bug was playing out in reverse!

Chapter 34

A FRENCH CONNECTION

Our next stop was Akaroa, which is the only French settlement in New Zealand, and was founded by settlers in 1840. As Catherine studied in Paris, and loves the French language, she was fascinated to find out how much it still retained a French influence, and was delighted to discover many French-speaking residents as well as quaint French-influenced shops that reminded her of small towns in France.

We stayed in a spotless little boutique bed and breakfast, built in 1859, where the unique lounge extended over a stream below. We told the owner how we had discovered her in our precious, trusty guide book and immediately chose her home at the head of Akaroa Harbour; it was near the waterfront, shops and cafes, and the one main street that skirts a bay famous for its visiting dolphins. Seats were dotted around the flower garden and by the brook – for peaceful contemplation.

Our hostess recommended eating in Bully Hayes' restaurant, named after a notorious American pirate of days gone by. We made our way through their taster menu, then sat outside admiring stately yachts of every dimension pass right in front of us, and toying with which one we would buy if we won the lottery.

'I could chat up one of the owners for an invitation on board,' suggested Catherine, but I'm not sure if they would take you, Mum ...."

'Well, make sure you take the scenic route,' said the guy. 'It's much more interesting. Avoid the coast'.

Little exchanges like this were already making our trip special. Catherine did the driving and I was the navigator as we cruised inland up the Waitaki Valley, passing through Omarama and seeing Lake Aviemore on the way. It was all lakes in this area: in one day we passed Lake Pukaki and stopped at Little River Cafe on Lake Tekapo for lunch.

Chapter 35

BACK IN THE 1930'S

Having driven through the fields and vineyards we took the ferry to the North Island, and as we sailed into Wellington harbour, picked up our hire car, we were still wondering what differences to expect.

Courtney Place, Wellington, was a buzzing hive of cafés and bars, and the city immediately impressed us as classy. The stylish old-world Cambridge hotel was full of backpackers, including plenty of mature people, which surprised me.

There is a fair amount of Art Deco architecture on the south coast where I live, but I didn't expect to be visiting the Art Deco capital of the world here. We just happened to land in Napier during its annual Art Deco Week. It's an internationally acclaimed festival that began in 1931, in the worst depths of the Great Depression, after Napier was levelled to the ground by an earthquake and subsequent fires. It was rebuilt in only two years, at the height of Art Deco fashion, so nowhere else in the world will you find so many stylish 1930's buildings. The present-day residents have Art Deco in their bloodstream.

Luckily, we had booked in advance at Archie's Bunker hostel, on a quiet street near Napier Museum. Doug and Julie have personalized this stopover with their friendly local knowledge, offering tips about everything of possible interest. Some people stayed with them for weeks.

Once settled in to our digs, we walked straight out into the middle of a vintage car parade. Drivers and spectators were dressed up in period costumes; flapper-style dresses and Gatsby suits. Except for us, every resident was in character, and we even passed a shop specialising in 1930s' accessories: hats, scarves, gloves, braces, spats, dress jewellery and walking canes to embellish the outfits.

Volunteer-guided architectural tours were booked up, all profits being used to maintain and restore the buildings, but it really didn't matter as the 1930s engulfed us. Every street was festooned in colourful lights and balloons and festival participants heartily encouraged us to immerse ourselves in the atmosphere. We had sailed into the right place at the right time for a fabulous experience. A couple of alcohol shots helped us overcome our inhibitions and throw ourselves into the street dancing, from which we rolled back to the hostel at one in the morning!

A couple at breakfast had come from Taupō, which happened to be our next stop and they warned us about the exceptionally winding drive that had frequent steep climbs. By leaving early, we would avoid the sun in our eyes, which was useful information.

'It's over to you for the driving then,' I told Catherine., as I'm not great on snaking mountain roads. She agreed on condition I didn't hold onto the dashboard and ask her to slow down. 'And look out for that sign they told us about on the Taupo Road ... of those spectacular waterfalls.

'That's going to be your job, Mum' she said, firmly placing the ball in my court.

So, we revved up the car, prepared not to be traumatized by daunting bends and precipitous climbs. We found our fellow guests had been correct on every detail. The spectacular Waipunga Falls are among the highest in the country and definitely merited the detour. One main fall split into three as it descended and we were taken aback by the power of the water. We would have easily missed the turn-off without some idle chatter over the breakfast table.

Our next stop was Rainbow Lodge, next to Taupo's famous Huka Falls. The falls gush into a lake of turquoise water, Lake Taupō, which pours into a narrow strip and then cascades down the mountain. Standing on the bridge, we could feel the vibrations made by the heavy torrents gushing under our feet, the soft humidity of the spray and could have stood enraptured by its hypnotic spell indefinitely. I have never before heard such a drumming thunder of water. Like hovering eagles, we saw tiny people on a boat ride far below, taking pictures from the swirling pools as if they were white-water rafting. The cascade was a stirring display of natural power and, for the first time, I realised just how *blue* blue could be. Up in the sky, intertwined rainbows were sparkling in the sunshine, which must have been a common sight captured as it was in our B&B's name, Rainbow Lodge.

We were brought back to reality next day with a four-hour drive north to Auckland via Thame formerly known as Thames, when two settlements were merged to support local 19th century gold-mines, but known as *Hauraki* to its Māori predecessors and its present inhabitants.

The strong Indigenous culture was clearly in

evidence in the central parts of North Island. The Māori peoples came originally from Polynesia, discovering New Zealand as they navigated the Pacific Ocean by the stars and currents in Arawa canoes. These large double-hulled boats, built over seven hundred years ago, carried several migrations of Indigenous people who settled peacefully in this part of North Island.

As rugby fans, we had seen the New Zealand All-Blacks Rugby team performing the energetic *haka* ritual before international games, and were excited to understand more about Māori culture. *The tradition of hak*, which is expressed in many forms goes way back into Māori mythology and was originally danced as an emotional celebration of life, in honour of creation myths, or offering a welcome to illustrious guests. Christian missionaries attempted to discourage haka ceremonies, but twenty years after it was performed for the Duke of Edinburgh in 1869 the New Zealand native football team tour publicly embraced their tradition, and it has been adopted by the national All-Blacks team ever since 1905.

Modern historians recognise four overlapping cultural eras that contribute to *Maoritanga*, Maori culture, from around 1200 AD, through to the 19th century, when Maori began to interact with European settlers after the 1840 Treaty of Waitangi was signed between the British Crown and Maori Chiefs. The Waitangi Treaty promised to respect, protect and enable Maori people to remain and thrive in New Zealand and, although claims about land, fishing, language, pollution and education are ongoing at the Waitangi Tribunal, the treaty still exists today.

In this modern era, Maoritanga has been shaped by increasing urbanization and closer contact with European settlers, but also with revival of traditional practices. Māori arts or carving, weaving, group performances, oratory and tattoo play a large role on the New Zealand arts scene, which is captivated by the patterns, stories and characters through which Māori artists record and communicate their history, genealogies and beliefs. This was the legendary South Pacific, just the other side of the ocean from where Maori explorers had navigated from Polynesia in carved tree boats during our Middle Ages.

From our accommodation in Mayfair Lodge, we sauntered along the Pacific coast and noticed posters advertising trips to the islands. We joined a boat trip to the Hole in the Rock as two of only ten passengers who were regaled by Pete, the skipper, filling us in on the landscape and telling us more about the orcas (killer whales) and penguins who were cavorting either side of the boat. The skipper dropped anchor for us at the Hole in the Rock, a weather-eroded arch, and he invited us to try the hazardous climb to its summit to benefit from an exhilarating view. We had fun wading from the back of the boat through a turquoise sea to the spotless white sands. My fellow passengers climbed it, but you know about me and heights, I was too pre-occupied with imagining I'd fall and smash against the base of the rock – not an ending I wanted to my quest.

Instead, I stood on the idyllic, tropical beach, feeling the sand caress my toes and replaying the love scene in *"From Here to Eternity"* where Sergeant Milton Warden (Burt Lancaster) and army wife Karen Holmes (Deborah Kerr) lay entangled in the wash oblivious to the surge of the tide over their adulterous embrace. The warm blue ocean swelled into crests of white foam, as waves washed over them and crashed onto the sand. This highly symbolic scene had been considerably toned down from the source novel, in line with 'acceptable family viewing' for the 1950's audience. Even so, I was not allowed to see it as I was only about nine years old. It was many years later, when it was shown in our local cinema, that I had the pleasure of finding out what all the fuss was about! How times have changed!

Back on board, Catherine was deep in conversation with a young English couple, who we joined for a drink before parting company. We sailed happily back via Russell, which looked enticingly quaint, so agreed on a regular ferry in the morning to investigate. It was early evening before we docked in Paihia, and I was a bit jaded, so after a single glass of wine I left Catherine to make her way back when she was ready.

Our hunch about Russell was well justified. There we found the tiniest and oldest church in New Zealand; beautiful and steeped in history. Charles Darwin contributed towards building it, and the graveyard contained intriguing historical monuments dating back to the 1840s. Throughout the mid 19th century many conflicts arose between the European settlers and the Maori people and musket holes in the walls of the church bore witness to the Battle in 1845. *Kororareka* means 'how sweet is the penguin' but it was renamed 'Russell', which seems far less romantic. A plaque mounted, over a century later, commemorates Queen Elizabeth II and Prince Philip's visit when they honoured the Maori people. The nineteenth century also saw the arrival of American and European whaling ships, which we learned about in the Russell Museum before sauntering around the pretty shops, feeling smug to have been up and out early.

Piha is on the Tasman Sea. *The Piano* was filmed on Piha's fine surfing beach, *Karekare*; notably, the scene where the ship is grounded and the piano taken off the boat and deposited on the beach. I reimagined that scene: the mother playing sonorously at her piano while her daughter performed cartwheels on the sand.

We were meeting Jason in a coffee shop and following him to their family home next to the beach. Dale was at the front door holding their beautiful son Adam in her arms to welcome us. We heard about their wedding and their new life since they returned to New Zealand and they asked about Siobhan.

'How about spending your last five days in New Zealand here with us? That is, if you haven't got better plans?' suggested Dale.

We were thrilled to accept their generosity of spirit.

We all hit the road next morning for Kitekite Falls, where three layers tumble into a swimming hole. Together we drifted along Piha beach, choosing one of many tracks that led to steps right up to the fall. The little family regularly swam in the pond and picnicked at the top. From there we drank in a thirst-quenching view of the rainforest, then swam under the bracing cold falls, which was undeniably exhilarating. It felt special to be shown this hidden gem, which does not feature in tourist books, and to spend the morning soaking up its singularity.

After lunch, we took a satisfied stroll back along the beach and home for a nap. Dale's parents lived nearby and had invited us for dinner. They treated us as if we had known them forever. I immediately understood why Jason and Dale wanted to make their home surrounded by this idyllic way of life, rather than the hustle and bustle of London.

Catherine and I slept like babies, and were fresh and ready for our lone hike on the Waitakere Ranges' signposted trails.

'You're on duty today, Fred! Exercises in the mountains.'

'About time... I need some action. Like Ruby said, 'these boots are made for walking!' I tried to laugh – honestly, I did.

First, we looked in at *Arataki*, a visitor's centre that lived up to its Maori name meaning 'place of learning'. The guide there pointed out that it would take weeks to cover the whole mountain area, even if we did avoid getting lost! However, he matched us to tracks that suited our experience and fitness levels, and offered the option of taking along a guide. We chose the least complicated track, on our own, and took a well-designed route map. The route was well marked, and walking it felt like paradise. Indeed, the only track we lost was of the time as we grew more and more intrigued by the unfamiliar flora and fauna so close to the city of Auckland. Jason welcomed us home with food, wine, and enthusiasm to hear about our day.

By contrast, Dale took us to Auckland next day for a taste of the city, which residents charmingly call the City of Sails.

We packed in all we could, including panoramic views from Mount Victoria, and returned to a dinner invitation, this time from Jason's parents, who wanted to quiz us on how we found their country. We tried to express how overawed we were, left breathless by the landscapes and the friendliness of the people we'd met. His mother was a fantastic cook and we passed a really enjoyable few hours with them. Dale and Jason visibly relished being close to their parents and I quietly pondered whether that felt unfair to Catherine, having lost her father. Jason recognised that the quality and pace of life they enjoyed here would be difficult to equal, let alone surpass, anywhere else, so why wouldn't they rear their family where they were reared? We totally agreed with them.

On our last full day, we picnicked on a different track in the Waitakere Ranges, and set up a discussion about what it would be like to live here. An experienced windsurfer or a strong swimmer wouldn't be put off by the elements, but the Tasman Sea certainly demanded a lot of respect. It looked enticing enough but we were warned not to be fooled into thinking it is as friendly as it looks. That evening Dale invited *both* sets of parents for a farewell dinner, making us quite sad to be leaving our new friends who had given such heart to our stay and who we would have loved to know better. We agreed how easy we felt among such a close-knit family, not outsiders at all, and I felt renewed gratitude for being so close to my family too. We felt as if we had left the best to last.

And when we next opened our eyes, it was to brace ourselves for multiple goodbyes. It was goodbye to Jason and Dale; but, more poignantly still, Catherine was flying back home to Heathrow while I was setting off solo for Honolulu via Sydney. Today stood out as the first time since Hong Kong that I would have given my eye teeth to be going home with Catherine and not travelling alone.

'I'll never *ever* forget our time here together, Mum' said Catherine, as she wrapped her arms around me. We hugged tight, neither of us wanting to say goodbye, and as stoic as we tried, we could not hold back our tears.

Ruby was emotional too. 'I wish you weren't leaving Rita. I'll miss having someone who understands what it's like being the dogsbody! Perhaps we will cross paths again.... back home?' You never know...' And she broke off, sobbing.

'Typical rucksacks!' grumbled Fred. 'What would happen if we boots started crying?"

Our long-planned and dreamed of adventures had flashed by. It was only yesterday that I met my zombied Catherine, on this same spot. My eyes welled up at seeing her turn and walk away from me through the departure gate.

Chapter 36

RE-IMAGINING PEARL HARBOUR

Happily, there was only a short wait before I boarded for Honolulu. Just enough to dwell on New Zealand's beauty and to set my intention to return.

One day, before I self-identified as a globe-trotter but was beginning to moot the idea, I was playing golf with my friend Pauline.

'Why not fly from New Zealand to Honolulu and spend a week with Katherine and me? It's silly not to... it's on your way to Florida,' she said.

'We'll be staying there with Carolyn.' And, as if I needed my arm twisted, she added, 'We could get in some golf too!'

I went back to Pauline's for coffee, showed her my itinerary, and right there and then we picked a week at the end of February for the Honolulu meet-up!

'No problem with that idea, Brigid' Grainne

reassured me. 'You can break your journey on a round-the-world-ticket.'

So, with that encouragement, we firmed up some stopovers. I dovetailed in Chicago for St. Patrick's Day, and decided on our apartment in Florida as a grand finale. The revised plan worked perfectly.

And suddenly there I was, in Honolulu. The Hawaiian archipelago, in the North Pacific Ocean, consists of a hundred and thirty-seven islands. Its first Polynesian settlers arrive in the 8th century and, on 21st August 1959, Hawaii became the fiftieth state in the union of the United States of America. I had travelled half way round the world to meet Pauline and Katherine, friends from my neighbouring village.

They were there to meet me and we were all excited. After lots of teary hugs we set off for Carolyn's house where we would be staying. I had met Carolyn in England the previous year when she was visiting her two longtime friends. Carolyn and Katherine have wonderful singing voices, especially for spiritual music, which was how they met. Carolyn introduced her husband Brad, a colonel in the US air force who was stationed here at Hickham Airforce Base. Straightaway he asked if we fancied a game of golf at the air force base the next day. He didn't have to ask twice!

True to his word, our names were at the checkpoint. Carolyn showed her ID credentials and we showed our passports. An exciting start. From then on, we were VIPs. Carolyn and Katherine hung around, to lunch with us later, while we two players signed in at the clubhouse and donned our shoes. Our clubs were loaded onto a golf cart and we were off.

It felt as if we were playing on our own private course. As we drove onto the first tee we looked out over the sea, with spectacular surrounding landscapes. We didn't see another player out there, only airplanes swooping over our heads as they took off and landed. It was surreal! We spent most of our time admiring the scenery instead of concentrating on our golf. Well, who could blame us? It was such a unique opportunity.

After a substantial lunch in the beautiful dining room, we were taken to the NAAFI, which was the biggest Cash 'n' Carry I had ever seen; like a huge aircraft hangar. Maybe it was? You could buy anything there: food, clothing, furniture, electrical goods, you name it they had it! It reminded me of a massive Walmart or Costco with generous discounted prices, but triple the size! 'Christmas every day' is how I thought of it.

I only discovered that pineapples grew in the

ground until that Saturday morning when we visited the Dole Pineapple Plantation, named after the Dole family, from which Stanford B Dole became President of Hawaii in 1894. The growing crop looked like rows and rows of potato drills, but the pieces of pineapple we were offered had the best ever flavour. I have never, before or since, tasted pineapple as good as this. In fact, I am spoiled for it. None of the fruit I eat these days is anywhere near as flavoursome as the pineapple I tasted in Hawaii.

On our way back, we stopped at The Halona Blowhole, a spectacular sight formed thousands of years ago by volcanic activity in Oahu, when Koko Crater's lava flowed into the ocean during the Honolulu Volcanics' activity around 7,000 years ago. The lava tubes were narrow at the top but extended all the way out into the sea. A narrow rift along the cliff base was created by a large section of rock that broke away from the mainland.

On windy days, when the tide is high, ocean breezes send the waves crashing into shore where the rock formation then shoots sea-spray high into the air through the cave, acting like a geyser. These blowholes are most active when the tide is high and the winds are strong. They can shoot sea water thirty feet into the air. Below Halona is one of the most dangerous ocean currents in the world due to the Ka Iwi Channel; too many fatalities have resulted from people straying close to the edge, so we were happy to stay at the safe distance of a viewing platform.

Millions of years of volcanic eruptions not only fashioned the Hawaiian archipelago, they continually transform its landscape. Most lava flows towards the ocean, but occasionally it heads inland so that islanders have to take refuge in churches, shelters or with neighbours, as they watch cracks and vents open up beside and beneath their homes. The most recent eruption was in May 2018, making this an ever-present threat to life and livelihood.

On Sunday, Carolyn and I headed off for the usual Mass, but I found it hard to engage with the ritual because I kept thinking of the highly-publicised longtime sexual abuse of children by priests in the diocese. It was in the Honolulu press, radio and on TV throughout my stay. So, Mass did not leave me in a cheerful or elevated mood. Instead, I came away feeling angry and ashamed.

Having been cosseted by others until now, I wanted to establish some independence and booked a six-hour tour to Pearl Harbour for the following morning. But I was still feeling subdued when I woke and, although I expected a sombre trip, was not prepared for the profound emotions Pearl Harbour would bring up for me. We were introduced to the topic by a powerful documentary about the Japanese attack, with footage relating the weeks leading up to it, followed by the actual day's events that left me overawed by sorrow, helplessness and dread.

I left the screening room with my head spinning around the atrocity of wars, and have never forgotten that sensation. *Those men on board ships in Pearl Harbour never stood a chance... like sitting ducks...* In that subdued mood, we were ferried across the bay to the *USS Arizona* Memorial where we were told stories by survivors of the catastrophic day about their shipmates' bravery and sacrifice. It was a harrowing session that left me crying with pity. To compound the despair, we continued by exploring the decks and interior of the *Battleship Missouri*, which was active in ending World War II, and acted as a vivid visual prompt of the men's living conditions.

I lost enthusiasm for sightseeing after that, so returned to Pauline and Catherine.

'You look like you've lost your best friend!' said someone, as I walked in.

The more I regaled them with my disturbing reactions, the more they realised they could have warned me. They had come away in exactly the same state. It was a sobering lesson for us all to dwell on.

On the last day with my golfing friends, we went out to the roadside waterfalls which were in full flow, causing some blowholes to spout very dramatically. We climbed the long-dormant Diamond Head crater to see the sun set, and we peered into its cavernous interior. For my farewell dinner, Carolyn and her husband took us to Oahu's revolving restaurant, famous as the opening scene of the TV series *Hawaii 5-0*.

And then we saw the whales!

It was my last memory: a pod of whales, in clear focus, cavorting in the setting sun and generating a matchless climax to this still-haunting scene.

Ruby was stuffed full for another goodbye in another airport. This time, on board, she sat on the floor beside Fred so she was a happy piece of canvas. She wriggled around and settled comfortably into airline mode. I fastened my seatbelt, all set for Maui in the Central Pacific.

My week in Honolulu was chock-full with the power of the natural world, and with the over-riding sadness of Pearl Harbour – a sensation that lives on in my heart. My next stop would be with Shirley and

John, in Maui.

Michael and I had met these old friends on a golf course in Florida many years earlier. We had an instant rapport and they loved Michael's dry Irish wit. Those were happy days and our friendship lasted all these years, including staying at each other's homes on holidays.

They were distraught to hear of Michael's death, especially as he had missed out on his once in a lifetime wish to attend the US Open Golf Championship, which was finally to be played on their home course of Shinnecock Hills, Long Island.

The invitation had arrived as he was lying in his hospital bed, and there were dreadful moments since when I berated that he hadn't the good grace to stay alive until the tournament.

'Your timing's bad, Michael,' I had teased, in every expectation of his complete recovery. 'It's inconsiderate of you to be ill now, of all times.'

'Not exactly a bed of roses for me either... I didn't choose this option!'

Well, one of us made it here. Just the one.

As soon as I appeared from the Customs Hall, Shirley ran over and placed a garland around my neck in a traditional greeting of welcome and John followed it up with a bear-hug. The orchids, strung together as a symbol of love and friendship, nestled snugly around my neck and made me feel quite special.

'It's tickling!' said Ruby. 'And I might be getting hay fever... a-aa-aaah-tishoo!'

I didn't have the inclination to bless her.

'No luggage?' asked Shirley.

'What does she think I am then? Scotch mist?'

After a leisurely breakfast Shirley and John suggested visiting nearby Lahaina town, whose name means 'relentless sun'. It was a compact place, historic as a whaling port, and with an old-style vibe: plenty of art galleries and quirky shops, and the island's largest Banyan tree that shades the town square from the eponymous 'relentless sun'. We lunched at Kimo's, admiring the stunning mountain scenery and watching yachts bob high and low on the ocean, then ambled along Kaanapali beach to watch the sun set.

Lahaina, set as it is in Maui's warm waters, is the most active winter playground for humpback whales. Whale watching season was in full swing and getting up close I was astounded to see how gigantic these creatures really are, and yet they are muscular and agile enough to jump out of the water.

As we relaxed into the evening, Shirley shared her lasting memory of Michael, of an unforgettable occasion when she was teeing off and he was in critical mode.

'Shirley, you're not following through with your swing!' he proffered.

'Yes, I know you're right Michael' she conceded.

'I know I'm right – I'm always right... *but it's not easy!*' came his now legendary retort.

'Remember Michael's *"It's not easy!"*? she asked me.

'Shirley, how could I ever forget?' Those words had become synonymous with Michael.

'Playing golf has never been the same without him,' she told me. 'That catch-phrase of his is indelibly etched on my mind every time I forget to follow through on my swing!'

I am continually amazed and delighted to meet up with old and new friends on my journey. But, with a flutter of wings, my departure day for Chicago had arrived. Our time together had felt curtailed, as if we had so much more to share, and I wondered if we would ever meet up again. A bittersweet sensation permeated the pit of my stomach as these dear friends and I waved goodbye to each other.

Chapter 37

A SEA OF GREEN

Why Chicago? It was certainly an abrupt change from the heavenly Pacific islands, but I had long intended to be part of their annual St Patrick's Day celebrations and attend the world's most lavish show of Irish fervour outside the Emerald Isle; a parade I had heard about all my life. This year was *my* year!

When Grainne was arranging my flights, she offered three alternative stops to choose from between Hawaii and mainland USA. And there on the list was Chicago, waving the green, white and gold tricolour at me. At last, a chance to take up the long-standing invitation from Harry and Grace. I was excited at the prospect.

'When we're at the St Patrick's Day Parade, Ruby, you'll be carrying the Irish flag for us!' I told her.

'And what do I get?' demanded a curmudgeonly

Fred.

'Well... how about some emerald green socks?' That made him happy.

Grace was a bohemian with a terrific sense of humour. She was headmistress of an elite girls' school and had endless anecdotes about school life. Harry was a lifelong journalist and political analyst for the *Chicago Tribune*. He had a distinctive, eloquent speaking voice and I could listen to his stories all day long! Amongst other claims to fame, he was first to interview John F Kennedy on the day he was elected president. A framed photo of the event took pride of place over their fireplace. Ironically, Harry also covered JFK's assassination. He reminded me a lot of Walter Cronkite, another American broadcaster and long-standing anchorman for CBS Evening News. More importantly, he had a golf swing to die for!

Before setting foot out of England, I rang them to say I was finally making it to Chicago and to check if their invitation was still on the table. Harry had answered the phone.

'I'm so sorry, Brigid... very sad news...' he faltered. 'Grace died... last year... a terrible accident.'

He steadied himself and went on to explain.

'She'd made a cake... putting it in the oven...' He hesitated. Even though he must have rehearsed the story so many times, he still found it hard to articulate. 'Grace... she went to light the gas and... it ignited in a ball of fire... she was burnt everywhere... face, body...'

I felt the shock rise up through me.

'I'm sorry to have to say it, Brigid... but she didn't survive her injuries.' I could feel the pain in his voice and was lost for words. How to respond to news like that?

I was silent as he went on to say he would love us both to stay with him in Chicago. And then it was my turn. I inhaled deeply and shared the circumstances of how Michael too had died the previous year.

'Brigid, you'd be doing me a favour to stay here for the week. Let me show you around. It'll be something good to look forward to.'

What to say? I was reeling with shock about Grace, but accepted his offer. Now at least he had a new project, planning sightseeing for me, including the St Patrick's Day festivities. Knowing him as I did, he would make my stay memorable. I gave him the details of my flight, and it was fixed. I was going to spend a week with Harry.

I disembarked the eight-hour flight from Honolulu to Chicago, and that afternoon at O'Hair Airport, time stood still. There was Harry, a larger-than-life character at six foot six, wearing a huge smile and clutching a bouquet of flowers to welcome me. We embraced in a long bittersweet hug.

'If only Grace was here... to greet you...' he stammered. And we both broke down in tears, struggling to regain enough composure to set the tone for the week. It was hard for us to see each other, as we were endlessly conscious of our times as a foursome with Grace and Michael.

'I'm going to give you a great time from both of us... even though I can't cook... or make a mean gin and tonic like my Grace.' He had broken through our sorrow and we chuckled.

Oak Park had once been voted the World's Largest Village and has a reputation for being the best place to live in Illinois. It is in the Italian district of the city and Harry gave me a little guided tour on the way to his home. Every house in their tree-lined avenue was individual in style and design, and we passed opulent mansions belonging to Italian Mafia families. The double fronted home they had shared was of Victorian design and sported stained glass windows above the door. Architecture was king here, and the homes of Frank Lloyd Wright and Ernest Hemingway were within walking distance – both now curated as museums.

Harry had left a bottle of champagne chilling in an ice-bucket to help celebrate our meeting after so long. I tried my best to comfort him over Grace and think my company helped him to reminisce about those days we all spent together on Longboat Key, Florida. I felt an inevitable pang of remorse at not having made the effort to visit when she was alive, but that is how life catches you out and none of us can wind back the clock.

Harry had put together a fantastic plan for me and unmistakably wanted me to reap the best of Chicago. Firstly, we went for lunch at Marshall Fields, a prestigious department store with an elegant oak-panelled restaurant on the top floor. It made me think of London's Harrods or The Savoy.

Harry usually took a nap in the afternoon, so we went back home.

'Actually, I'm rather a dud cook. Would you mind if we eat out again tonight?'

'But I remember your famous shrimp parties in Florida!' I reminded him.

'Haha! There's a trick to that,' he said. 'I didn't have to cook anything... everyone peeled their own shrimp and helped themselves to ready-made salads.

I just refilled your glasses!'

So, that evening we ended up at Smith and Wollensky, an old-established steak house, where we reminisced some more. It did us good.

On Sunday, Harry directed me to the Catholic church at the end of his street.

'Keep an eye out for the large limos... the ones with the bodyguards wielding sub-machine guns standing next to them,' he said. 'They'll be protecting their bosses as they walk into pray!'

He was referring to the Italian Mafioso who attended Mass every Sunday morning. I noticed that the front pews were all empty, possibly being reserved for the Mafia families. I toyed with the idea of wandering up and occupying a front seat but, being a coward, I resisted the urge.

I passed some massive homes on my way to and from church, lavishly (dare I say 'garishly'?) adorned, and with marble staircases leading to imposing front doors where serious-looking men stood on either side with guns. It would not take a rocket scientist to work out who lived there. The houses stuck out like their wealthy owners, and no one could accuse them of being understated; each tried to outdo the other with its opulence. A bonus of Harry living in that street was that his home had never been burgled!

'Fancy a break from the big city?' Harry suggested after a slow breakfast. 'We could drive to Milwaukee, and see some countryside?' It was an appealing idea.

Milwaukee is home to the German Miller Brewing Company, which makes the world-renowned *Miller Lite* beer. We took a guided tour around Miller's, where simply the smell of the hops made me feel intoxicated. It is an important centre for NASCAR stockcar races, as well as being home of the Harley Davidson, with a motorcycle museum to prove it! Milwaukee's Summerfest is the major music festival in Michigan state, so the place is filled with a certain music buzz even out of season and big stars have been accommodated in its concert venues including Bon Jovi, The Beatles, Def Leppard and Bruce Springsteen.

While Harry stopped off at a café I ambled, in shining sun, along the riverside boardwalk of this different Michigan lakefront. I could have walked for miles along its sandy beach, feeling more at the seaside than by a lake.

But I tore myself away from the lakeside and meandered in towards the old-fashioned buildings in 3rd Street. Milwaukee was a complete contrast after craning my neck at Chicago's massive modern skyscrapers. I discovered the Wisconsin Cheese Mart, a family-owned store with a vast array of local and international cheeses, sausages and sauerkraut. There is a significant German immigrant community, dating back to the 1840s, and I saw long queues, of mostly tourists, outside Maters, the town's oldest established German restaurant. Instead, Harry and I chose a farm-to-table eatery that served local craft beers.

We headed home from Wisconsin State before the evening traffic. I did offer to share the driving, but he was old school and said that I was his guest and he was more than happy to chauffeur me. As we neared Chicago, a stark comparison hit me between the quiet pace of life we had left and the hustle of Chicago! I realised how much it mattered to experience both urban and rural areas.

At last St Patrick's Day arrived – and what a hoot! The first thing I did was to attend a traditional St Patrick's Day Mass in St Mary of the Angels church, which is modelled on St Peter's Basilica in Rome. To confess, I spent the Mass admiring some of the finest specimens of Roman Renaissance church architecture I have ever seen, plus multiple paintings, sculptures, stained-glass windows and a huge pipe organ. But, when the organist began to play 'Hail

Glorious St Patrick', I could not help dropping a tear; it was so moving and I was instantly transported to my Irish childhood.

'What's up?' asked Harry, seeing my tear-stained face.

I told him how homesick I felt at hearing St Patrick's hymn being so beautifully arranged and kind-heartedly he put his arm around me.

'Cheer up... you're in for an exciting day. The Irish communities have got a huge influence here in Chicago. Plenty of the mayors originated from Irish immigrants.'

In the 1840's over 1,000,000 Irish people were forced to emigrate by the Potato Famine and many came to the new growing city of Chicago until by 1850 they made up a fifth of its population. Folk in Chicago really know how to celebrate their feast day with passion; Harry certainly got that right! I harnessed my nostalgia and went to mingle in the throngs of people watching the parade. Everywhere we looked was green.

'Brigid... you're not going to paint me green too, are you?' Ruby asked, as we got ready.

'No, then you wouldn't be Ruby any more... Ha...! I'd have to call you Esmeralda.' It was one for her to think about. 'But I am going to stick a tricolour flag in you!'

'I don't want to be trampled on by those crowds. Piped up Fred. Can I stay home and have a day off?'

'No, you can't, Fred! After I've bought you special green socks...'

'Okay. I suppose it's the least I can do,' he sighed.

By noon, Columbus Drive was heaving with thousands of young people, old people, children, dogs – all dressed in green costumes and some wearing shamrock on their lapels. Masses were waving the Irish flag of green, white and gold, and even the Chicago River had been dyed emerald. A catching sense of anticipation was building up and up, even before a first glimpse of the parade, and I felt proud to be Irish. It filled me with happiness to witness this outpouring of Irish love and patriotism.

'These folks don't have an Irish accent like you,' remarked Ruby. 'You sure you're at the right parade?' I ignored her, but it was a good observation for a rucksack.

The crowd roared at the first glimpses and noises of the approaching parade, and the cheering and flag waving soared into waves of crescendo as it snaked past each block of the jam-packed streets. Police and fire brigade bands led the march down Columbus Avenue playing patriotic melodies, while girls and boys in ornately-embroidered traditional kilts, aprons, shawls and blouses, danced reels, hornpipes and jigs on low-loaders. I flashed back to my school of Irish dancing in Kilkenny, where we were entered in the *feis*, a traditional dance competition. In my mind's eye I saw myself in my embroidered dress and remembered the gruelling hours of training! My chest was positively bursting with pride in my heritage.

I have rarely seen such a throng: people of all shapes and sizes had dyed their hair emerald green and were draped in the green, white and gold. Some African-Americans had dyed their flamboyant afros emerald green too. It was joyful to see that everyone was joining in the spirit of the day. All it lacked was Michael Flatley and his troupe giving us a performance of *Riverdance*. That would have been icing on the emerald green cake. A leprechaun must have waved their magic wand, because it was a glorious sunny day with a temperature in the mid-sixties; unusual for Chicago.

Countless pubs, run by Irish staff, served bacon and cabbage and green-coloured Guinness that flowed all day long. Chicago folk were nearly surpassing how we celebrate our Irish heritage back home in Ireland. All they needed to match our Irish pubs was a few Irish rebel songs, or the cacophony of fiddlers and accordionists tuning up before the session.

Sean, Siobhan and Catherine would have been thrilled, and were no doubt envious to have missed out on St Patrick's Day in Chicago. It is indelibly etched in my brain.

Harry joined me for a traditional Irish meal… with a Guinness to ease it down, of course. I climbed into bed singing *When Irish Eyes are Smiling*, and thought of Michael, who would have loved Chicago's enthusiastic festivities.

I invited Harry to Brighton so I could return his hospitality, but he had lost the zest for long hauls, especially without Grace by his side. I was at a loss for words to console him, but managed to kiss him a tearful goodbye before boarding my internal flight to Tampa in Florida, and knowing that this was the last time I would ever see him.

Standing on Columbus Avenue, Chicago, immersed in the intoxicating fervour of St Patrick's Day, triggered off a heap of remembrances that came back to me on the flight to Tampa.

Seeing the parade of dancing youngsters made me intensely aware of my Irish legacy. The girls, some no more than five years old, wore traditional ringlets. My mother started me at Irish dancing classes when I was five. Even then it was a fiercely competitive activity and my budding future never blossomed at dance school. Imagine feeling a failure at five. But at least I was saved from ignominy and mortification by not being made to continue.

The roots of Irish dancing can be traced back to the Celts and Druids who roamed Ireland before St Patrick introduced Christianity. The *feis* was an arts, culture and music celebration held by local Celtic communities, of which dancing was an integral part.

It all happened up on the Hill of Tara, seat of the High King of Ireland and epicentre of the ancient Celtic world, where a great annual assembly, or *aonach*, was held for law-making, funerals and festive games, possibly as far back as 1600–1800 BCE. *Feiseanna* are still held today, around the world, but these days they are simply showcases at which trophies and medals are won or lost for competitive dancing.

The most famous modern exponent of traditional Irish dancing is Chicago's Michael Flatley who created and choreographed *Riverdance* before taking it to the world stage when it was performed as the interval act at Dublin's 1994 Eurovision Song Contest. The mood was just right at that time and step dancing took the world by storm.

Music is central to Irish culture, and visitors are welcomed to join in alongside regulars at any pub session where musicians get together and play their instruments in an impromptu way. Other musicians might come along later, or someone might be inspired to dance a reel, a jig or a hornpipe, or sing along to the music. Sessions can carry on for hours while everyone lubricates their throat with on-tap Guinness or Irish whiskey.

I sat trying to recall dance steps and the words to the ballads of my childhood, and the truth rose in me of how I missed the relaxed banter and the *craic* when I left Eire for England. As I grow older, I am more homesick for the camaraderie and spontaneity of my Irish roots. Having mentally and physically relived a stirring fill of home culture, 3470 miles away from the Emerald Isle, I snapped out of my reverie. We were about to touch down in Tampa.

'Where the hell are we now?' spouted my little canvas friend. 'You are about to meet Constanza. So kindly find some manners in one of your pockets!' I insisted.

And there she was, my lovely friend, standing there with her radiant smile.

Chapter 38

BEING THERE WAS FATE

A weekend soon after Michael's funeral, Catherine came down to stay with me in Brighton.

'What are you going to do now, Mum?' she asked, tentatively.

'I don't really know,' I answered. And I didn't. I had no conceivable notion of the life that awaited me now.

Catherine was suffering as much as I was over the loss of her father, and she suggested we should not be living alone that winter but both go to Florida. It was a welcome thought, to be in the sun, but I realised quickly that I could not face seeing Michael's old friends at Siesta Key, not so soon. So, we compromised by renting an apartment on Anna Maria Island instead.

It is very different from Siesta Key, a quirky

place with an eclectic mix of people from multi-millionaires to hippies. That winter we went there together and first met Constanza and Hugh under unusual circumstances, having locked ourselves out of our apartment after a walk on the beach. There were the keys, tucked safely inside. Luckily for us, Constanza and Hugh were walking their Poodle and noticed our dilemma. Like Spiderman, Hugh climbed the drainpipe up onto our balcony and found an open door into one of the bedrooms. He got us out of a real fix, and as a 'thank you' we popped some wine around.

They lived in a Dutch-style house with Milou the Poodle, and Isaac the iguana. Yes, I do mean a massive iguana who was draped across the back of their lounge settee. He scared the life from me, but Catherine was braver and let Hugh drape Isaac around her shoulders as if they were lifelong friends.

And so, began a friendship with these two wonderful people. They had no children – Milou and Isaac were their children. They had met in Paris, at a party in the American Embassy. She was working for the IMF and he for the American Government, in Virginia. He never mentioned his work, so I have always assumed it was secret. During their conversation she had asked if he would take a bottle of French perfume back to America for her friend and he agreed to do it, but only if she went out for dinner with him! The romantic upshot was that they started dating and were eventually married.

Because they had spent many happy holidays on Anna Maria Island, that was where they made their home. Hugh would fly his own plane to Virginia every Sunday night and back to Florida every Friday evening. This perfect routine settled into a pattern over the years, until one fateful Sunday when their lives changed forever.

Catherine had returned to England the previous day, so Constanza telephoned to invite me for a girls' night in once Hugh had left for Virginia. We were enjoying the evening, watching a movie with our pizza and a couple of glasses of wine. Hugh generally called to let her know he had landed safely in Virginia.

By nine-thirty we had finished eating and started on the movie, when the phone rang.

'That'll be Hugh – just a moment...' she said.

He always called around this time. Every Sunday. But this particular Sunday it was not Hugh on the phone. It was the airport manager, asking if Mr. Bryant had left Sarasota airport as he had not logged off his flight plan. Constanza replied that she had last spoken to Hugh when he was ready to take off after refuelling in South Carolina. He had remarked on the beautiful clear night and said he was leaving for Langley, Virginia, his final stop.

She suggested that the manager check whether her husband's car or plane was in the hangar. The call eventually came through, saying that Hugh's car was still in the hangar from Friday. There was no sign of the airplane – or of him. The manager promised to call again as soon as he had more information. Constanza was concerned by this time and asked me to stay with her until he rang back. She did not want to be alone in case there was a problem, so, of course, I did. We sat… and sat, until the phone sounded at two-thirty. The airport had received a call from a local farmer saying that he saw a plane plummet into the woods near his land. She would get another call when any details became available. We dozed restlessly in our chairs, until we heard a firm knock on the door. I opened it to two policemen. It was 8 a.m. Was I Mrs. Bryant, they asked. No, I wasn't. They came in.

It was brutal. Hugh's plane had hit the trees in thick fog, and gone down as he was approaching the landing strip. They told us that he was already dead in the cockpit when they reached him. Neither of us will forget that morning as long as we live. It created a lifelong bond between us. We both lost our husbands without warning, But Constanza's startling loss was the crueller. Hugh was only forty-five years old, at the top of his career, and they had no children to fill the shocking void. At least I had my son, two daughters and grandchildren to comfort and support me when Michael went.

But today this smiling Constanza was at the airport to meet me from Chicago, and took me to her home for something to eat. In the end, I stayed over with her that night as she wanted every tiny detail of my travel anecdotes. Next morning, she dropped me off to settle at my apartment on Anna Maria before we breakfasted on the beach.

Once Ruby and I had unpacked I rang Nuala and John, my neighbours on Siesta Key, and explained how I did not feel brave enough to stay there this year. Nuala was free and offered to pick me up for lunch.

I was really pleased to see them, but they did not understand quite how I felt. How could they? Does anyone truly understand major loss unless they have been through it? We had met some years previously in Tenerife, and after our invitation to visit us at Siesta Key we became close. I had spent happy hours taking Spanish lessons from Nuala. After years living in Tenerife, she was completely fluent in Spanish, and she taught me to love the language too.

They drove me right near Siesta Key for lunch, in spite of what I had said, and then into Siesta Key Village for coffee. I had tried to explain over lunch why I could not bring myself to go there, but they genuinely didn't clock why I was renting on the next island.

And then, exactly what I had been trying to avoid happened: we ran into two of Michael's friends who offered me their condolences. I found it distressing, as I had known I would, because memories rushed back of our old life as a couple here at Siesta Key, and my mind was flooded with thoughts of the good times we might have lived through had he been with me today. But his friends did say how much he was missed by the AA community and by all those he had helped to stay sober. I had not realised his impact at the time, nor how highly he had been respected.

'Come and see what we've done to our apartment!' begged Nuala.

So, with unease and trepidation, I reluctantly agreed to see their newly refurbished place. They had done a beautiful job of remodelling it but, on the way, we walked past the apartment where Michael and I had spent such happy holidays.

I don't know how I fought back the tears or stopped myself from breaking down as we passed 'our' front door. I think John and Nuala were well-meaningly trying to break me in for my eventual return to the community, but it was far too soon and far too painful. After I had admired their interior decor they drove me back to Anna Maria Island, from where I called Constanza. She could tell something had upset me, and suggested hooking up for the evening. I was relieved not to sit alone pondering all those 'what ifs'.

Instead, we made plans for some fun while I was in Florida. Constanza's first suggestion was a visit to her brother and sister-in-law in Orlando. He had made a successful career organizing the various restaurants, banqueting halls and hotel food services for the Disney World Corporation. He invited us over for a few days and asked if I would like to visit the theme parks while I was there. I jumped at the prospect, and it worked well for Constanza too as she could catch up with the Colombian side of her family who were also in town. So, I landed a VIP pass that granted access to all three Disney World parks. Memories flooded back of our 25th wedding anniversary, when we took a four-week family holiday in America and gave the children the unforgettable experience of Disneyland. So, now, I could testify to sampling the head of catering's excellent cuisine and was given some insights into how they cater for 30,000 punters on a daily basis! I was more than a little envious of the set of culinary knives he uses for his job!

We met Constanza's older brother on his horse farm, where he bred dressage horses and small ponies for children's rides for Disney. It was a far cry from the usual farming life that I grew up with in Ireland.

Once back from the razzle and dazzle of Disney we drove up to The Villages, a community for over fifty-fives that is known as the 'swingers' capital of America' – no, I'm not joking! We spent a couple of nights there with her friends, Rob and Marie, but I hasten to report that I did not dip into the swinger scene! Instead, Rob, who was a talented impersonator, entertained us memorably on several occasions with his Elvis act. Purportedly (and who am I to disagree?) they only escaped to The Villages to miss the New York winter.

And slowly it dawned on me that I was ready

for Easter celebrations in my comfortable little home by the choppy English Channel. Over more tranquil days in Florida, playing golf, walking the beaches, snacking at the Seafood Shack, I felt an inner resilience creeping back. I lay with my head on the pillow on the final night of my travels knowing that in those six months since leaving London I had grown stronger.

Mission accomplished. I was ready to go home to my family. It was an exciting prospect to see the children again, although I was not looking forward to an empty silent home when I left them in London.

Once on the plane, and with a long flight ahead, I fondly acknowledged my two constant companions throughout this significant time: Ruby, my rucksack and Fred, my boots. We were both nearly turfed out of the business class lounge at Heathrow because she, Fred and I didn't look swanky enough. We may not have fitted the ticket of business class world travellers but we became best friends. Fred supported me over every inch of the road, even on days that his mood plummeted. Like a real friend, Ruby pulled me up when I needed a word in my ear, and in return I treated her and Fred as kindly as possible. After all, Ruby held everything I needed for those six months and my life depended on what was stashed in her compartments. She put up with being chucked into overhead lockers, flung into car boots and the luggage holds of buses, stuffed under seats on ferries; it's a miracle that she survived in one piece with only a few minor stains and a slightly worn undercarriage. I tried to count how many unpackings and repackings we had been through together as we crossed the globe. Sometimes it felt like preparing for a military deployment, but we elevated it to a fine art, and she hardly complained – well not a lot. Fred had not had a full dubbin wax since we left home, even though I had treated myself to several massages and Ruby to an infrequent laundering. And now, were they destined to sit forlornly in the bottom of my wardrobe contemplating their youthful adventures?

Before this final flight, Ruby had asked for a rest.

'Could we put the brakes on the packing, unpacking, chucking around? I'm not getting any younger you know.'

'Don't be silly,' I had gently scolded, 'We're still both young at heart.'

'Just a bit of R and R then?' she pleaded.

'Now we're seasoned travellers, I have the bug. I want to see more of the world, and I need you and

Fred to have my back... well, and my feet of course!'

'Brigid, you should come down to earth and enjoy the memories of our first trip.'

'Sorry, but rest well because you'll be coming with me, friends,' I said.

'She's not joking,' grouched Fred. 'You can tell when she's got a bee in her bonnet!'

'I'll always discuss my plans with you, and not put you in danger,' I promised. 'Fair do?'

'Fair enough,' they agreed.

'C'mon then, get your acts together.' I chivvied. 'We're going home.'

And so started our adventures in far flung places for another nine years.

Chapter 39

COMING HOME

Unbeknownst to me, my three wonderful children had got together to discuss how to play my arrival. They were rightly concerned about me coming back to an empty house in Brighton and how I might react to the loneliness and hushed silence when I opened the front door and walked in. None of them lived nearby, so I could not pop down the road for an impromptu dinner, but they had devised a plan to help me gradually come to terms with living alone.

I walked out of Arrivals to a banner being held aloft with the greeting 'WELCOME HOME' writ large. After such a long and independent absence, I was overwhelmed by mixed emotions to actually be with them, and we shared tears of relief and joy. There we were in the very place I had left from, and it seemed as if no time had passed since I travelled alone to

Heathrow. Although tired, I was too adrenaline-fuelled to sleep. That afternoon and evening passed in delight as we relished each other's company and I regaled my beautiful grandchildren with stories of the unbelievable fairytale places I had seen.

Amongst themselves, the family decided I should stay for the Easter holidays. I was thrilled, and unexpectedly relieved because it meant I could divide the time between each of my children and grandchildren. I could also check in with my old college friends. After all, I had so much to thank them for in terms of ideas and introductions and I felt sure they would grill me with questions. I was certainly not ready to return to Brighton until after Michael's birthday on 15th April. It was difficult enough not to be celebrating with him, but I was dreading his absence like a presence in our empty home. I felt supported and comforted that they understood I would need help through this stage. I knew I would face up to living alone, but had to cope with it at my own pace.

Sean stepped up to the plate and took on the mantle of 'head of the household'. He made all the difference and I can't credit him enough for taking over the helm and working out exactly how he could help me adjust. His first action was to make significant changes by replacing all the lounge furniture and redecorating the house in a different colour. He redesigned the bedrooms, moving items that he thought would make me unhappy.

'Mum,' he said, 'just retrieve them when you're ready... and strong enough.' Nothing was being moved forever. 'And as you settle in you can add your own personal touches.'

If his father was looking down on him, he would have been extremely proud. There was a certain irony, because when Sean worked alongside Michael, the clients referred to him as 'the boy'. It took them a while to consider him as 'the man', but eventually they did, and continued to do business with him for many years after Michael had passed away.

These thoughtful changes were pivotal. No longer would I have to gaze at the chair in which Michael fell asleep after his game of golf. Replacing that chair was the first step that allowed me to move on. This life alone would be unfamiliar and strange. I saw Sean in a fresh light and developed the deepest respect and admiration in addition to my love for him. It took my husband's death for the spotlight to shine on my son, who showed his strength and command even though he had lost a soulmate.

I made a lot of visits in the weeks I stayed in

London. The first reunion was with my mother-in-law, who, as I write, is approaching her 108th birthday and still lives independently in her own house. It shows you how tough these Irish women are!

And then came the long boozy lunch with my college associates at one of our favourite eateries. Our reunion kicked off with a welcome home toast of champagne, after which they reported how they had looked forward to reading my blog as I journeyed on and asked a million questions. In turn, I could report back on their ideas and introductions, especially telling Pat how Siew Sai had given me the most magical time in Singapore when I was still pretty vulnerable.

'Well, you can thank him in person!' she replied. 'Siew Sai's coming to London for business next month. Shall we book a dinner with him and David?'

And then came the day when I turned the key to our front door – no, *my* front door – in Brighton. I needed to reconnect with neighbours and be part of a community again; no longer on the move like a Nomad. No more looking for sanctuary. No more running. Maybe the neighbours imagined I had moved away. Joanna, who lives alone next door, was glad of my company and enthusiastically asked me in for a welcome home supper.

'Tell me all about your trip,' she asked, bravely.

'How long have you got, Joanna?' I replied. 'It'll take quite a while.'

'Let's do it in stages then,' she decided. 'Over several suppers...'

'That's a deal!' I agreed.

The only way forward was to keep busy and return to the fold in the shape of Our Lady of Lourdes Church, where I have kind and caring friends. I knew it would be hard even seeing the seat that Michael occupied for Mass. Even today I see him sitting there, and Sister Pauline from the convent comments from time to time on my smartly-dressed husband who sat in that pew every Sunday. She doesn't realise that I find this painful; she is just being honest and sharing a memory. Catherine kept me company at weekends, and I felt lucky belonging to a village church community who were towers of strength for me. There was invariably someone who understood what I might be going through.

As for the golf club, having kept in touch, I met my closest friends for a game of golf and dinner. I joined a walking group, then a bridge club. I could see it would be a busy summer; just what I needed. I set up activities; ways to reconnect with my new life as a widow.

By May and June, I was back playing with a group of eight women golfers who went away on annual trips each summer, which helped in keeping up my spirits. As arranged, I went to Pat's to see David and Siew Sai. He was his cheerful and ebullient self and we reminisced happily over all he made possible for me.

'We never got in that game of golf at your club!' I reminded him.

'Absolutely not!' he laughed. 'I wasn't having my reputation damaged... being thrashed by a woman!'

Walking has always been my way to keep fit and recharge my batteries. I looked forward to weekly walks in the countryside with the Mid-Sussex Ramblers. Not only were they a friendly bunch, but I discovered parts of Sussex I would never have found on my own. Despite a busy enough life, re-entering my empty house still jarred every time.

They say each cloud has a silver lining, and the ray of sun that shone on me took the form of my lovely daughter Siobhan who invited me to spend the summer in Nice with her and the children. It was the lifeline I needed in a now solitary life and could not have happened at a more opportune time.

'Stay as short or long a time as you like, Mum,'

she said. 'It'll build you up mentally. That way you'll feel more positive for winter back home.'

I was over the moon; another nurturing time to look forward to. I spent the whole summer by the pool, swimming, reading, strolling around Nice, visiting Provence's *villages perchés*, Monte Carlo, Beaulieu, Antibes and the lively market in Ventimiglia. The bonus was an opportunity to practice my rusty French and to reach out rather than dwell on my own predicament. At weekends her husband Niall flew over from London. Well, someone had to work to pay for the holiday! I worried that I was becoming too good at this way of living.

Siobhan and I had plenty of time to think about where I should spend the coming winter, and she reckoned I should handle Siesta Key sooner rather than later. I agreed that the longer I put it off the harder it would be, so I plucked up the courage and booked a flight to Florida, bracing myself for meeting old friends and doing everyday things like playing bridge or golf, dining out and the occasional opera, in between long walks on the beach.

Constanza met me in Tampa with an even warmer hug than last time. As the weeks crept by, I carved out a new routine and settled into it. Finally, despite a niggly feeling that I may not succeed without my stalwart friend and husband, I completed on the purchase of my own apartment on Siesta Key. Michael would have been very proud of me making this leap of faith!

Chapter 40

REFLECTIONS

From the known to the unknown.

With the loss of my dependable soulmate, Michael, I knew my path in life would change and I would need to change with it.

Without my knowledge, and wanting to surprise me, Michael had instigated my journey. A serendipitous meeting with Brenda (and her birthday invitation) showed me the first step. Strangers along the way smoothed my cautious interactions with the unknown.

Would I have braved this first step alone? No, I didn't have the strength until my daughters opened the gate to my path. They knew Michael had planned to break the habit of a lifetime and take me to Australia without any golf clubs. Their protection bequeathed me the earliest flutter of confidence for that first uncertain step, by saying 'Yes, I will' to Brenda. From that moment I would encounter twists and blind turns, sheer rockfaces to scale and turbulent rivers to wade through. I was equipped for obstacles by Grainne, a co-patriot who felt like a sort of mentor across the generations.

How much was fate? And how much was trust? My soulmate's lifelong presence was helping me along the way; by my side even after he had gone. Little by little, taking small steps, I began to deal with the grief, sometimes not even realising what was happening. Always somewhere very close, he showed me the way to broaden my vision and grow in confidence. I could hear him.

'You can do this!' he would say. 'One step at a time... just like me when I joined the AA fellowship.'

'You're right Michael,' I'd concede. 'How am I doing so far?'

'You know I'm right – I'm always bloody right!' he would tell me. 'And you're going great guns.'

Anticipation and hope were abundant, but sadness and fear were my early travelling companions. Every now and then, joy lifted its face towards me. The support and generosity of others supplied me with the courage to keep walking across the crevice-ridden unknown.

I handled the challenges on my path, at least until I was temporarily tripped up by Christmas and New Year dragging me into a dark hole. Even surrounded by excellent friends I fell into the depths of loneliness and despair.

'Why did you leave me Michael?' I asked, shifting the blame.

But there he was, perched on my shoulder. 'You know you're getting there. Keep going. I really am with you every step of the way.'

I climbed back into the saddle, broadened my shoulders, sensed my feet solidly grounded and felt Ruby, who had my back; and I rounded the next bend in the road as it came up to meet me.

At some point I stopped feeling sorry for myself and began to think about other people, like John and Constanza and Harry; how they felt too. I knew their sorrow was different from my own, but we had enough common humanity to allow me in so that I could understand their unhappiness. Maybe, I began to think, my garnered strength would one day allow me to offer encouragement to others on their intrepid journeys through grief. Did those friends carry butterflies with them around every turn? Mine had become such constant companions that I scarcely noticed them until one day I awoke to feel an overwhelming calm, a stillness inside me. My butterflies had left on silent wings without so much as a goodbye. Maybe I had left some in Hong Kong International Airport as I breathed in and out in panic? Or were they flying with their tropical cousins, the Ulysses and the Cairn's Birdwing, in the Red Peak rainforest canopy?

On each new road and with every unfamiliar culture, I could feel my heart and mind actively expanding. I now know for sure that beyond every corner is another terrain to explore, a person to meet and understand, an endeavour that will teach me to stretch myself, an air that smells different from any other, or a pineapple that will never taste the same again. I froze, but then I drew breaths into my body and I thawed away the fear, growing in self-assurance and in a warm independence through which I gradually negotiated the route. And the path, when I look back at it, was not simply across continents or from generous friend to kind stranger.

The path I had trodden had gently led me from being a grieving widow to a self-reliant woman who had been blessed by love, and who was at peace with herself and the world, settled agreeably in her little home between the chalk cliffs and the hills.